The   es
to   w

Janet Marinelli
SERIES EDITOR

Sigrun Wolff Saphire
SENIOR EDITOR

Mark Tebbitt
SCIENCE EDITOR

Leah Kalotay
ART DIRECTOR

Joni Blackburn
COPY EDITOR

Steven Clemants
VICE-PRESIDENT,
SCIENCE &
PUBLICATIONS

Judith D. Zuk
PRESIDENT

Elizabeth Scholtz
DIRECTOR
EMERITUS

Handbook #181

Copyright © 2005 by Brooklyn Botanic Garden, Inc.

All-Region Guides, formerly *21st-Century Gardening
Series,* are published three times a year at
1000 Washington Ave., Brooklyn, NY 11225.

Subscription included in Brooklyn Botanic Garden
subscriber membership dues ($35 per year;
$45 outside the United States).

ISBN # 1-889538-66-3

Printed by Science Press, a division of the Mack
Printing Group. Printed on recycled paper.

Apples are one of the most popular fruits in the world, and with good reason: There are varieties
suited to the growing conditions in virtually all temperate regions.

The Best Apples to Buy and Grow

A Curious Tale: The Apple in North America

Tim Hensley

In 1905, the United States Department of Agriculture published a bulletin by staff pomologist W.H. Ragan, entitled *Nomenclature of the Apple: A Catalog of the Known Varieties Referred to in American Publications from 1804 to 1904*. This nearly 400-page compendium covers an era known to fruit historians as the golden age of American pomology, a period running from the presidency of Thomas Jefferson to the Wright brothers' liftoff at Kitty Hawk. It was a time of unparalleled public interest in new fruit varieties, when apples, pears, and peaches were critically reviewed and rated with the enthusiasm now reserved for Hollywood movies and popular music.

Ragan's *Nomenclature* lists 17,000 different apple names. Many of them are corrupted versions of the same name: 'Juniting', 'Juneting', 'Genneting', 'June-Eating', and 'Juneating White', for instance. Others are the inevitable nicknames that attach themselves to old or widely disseminated varieties: 'New York Pippin', 'Kentucky Red Streak', 'Illinois Red', 'Funkhouser', and 'Ben Davis', for example, are one and the same apple. But even allowing for overlap, the number of distinct varieties grown by Americans in the 19th century was somewhere around 14,000.

To the modern consumer used to apples that are sweet, round, and red, this number may seem enormously redundant. But in the 19th century, apples came in all shapes and guises, some with rough, sandpapery skin, others as misshapen as pota-

In the 19th century, roughly 14,000 apple varieties were grown in North America. Today, fewer than 100 varieties are commercially cultivated, and of those a mere handful dominate in grocery stores, chief among them 'Golden Delicious', 'Fuji', and 'Red Delicious', pictured here.

In 1629, Captain John Smith noted that peaches, apples, apricots, and figs "prosper[ed] exceedingly" in the Jamestown colony.

toes, and ranging from the size of a cherry to bigger than a grapefruit. Colors ran the entire spectrum with a wonderful impressionistic array of patterning—flushes, stripes, splashes, and dots. There was an apple for every community, taste, purpose, and season, with winter varieties especially prized. Apples were used for making cider, baking, drying, eating out of hand—even as livestock feed.

Compare all of this to the 90 or so varieties grown commercially in North America today, or to the handful of shiny cultivars on display at the local supermarket, and you are immediately faced with a pomological conundrum: How could Americans grow 14,000 different apples in the 19th century, and a hundred years later be conversant with only a few varieties, most notably, 'Red Delicious', 'Golden Delicious', and 'Granny Smith'?

What's more, while it is commonly held that the apple in your lunchbox, *Malus domestica*, is native to North America—Ralph Waldo Emerson once described the apple as "the American fruit"—it actually descends from imported, Old World stock. Shake on that tree for a while and you are confronted with an even greater riddle: If the apple is not native, how did Americans come to grow some 14,000 varieties by the end of the 19th century?

Considering furthermore how these two questions run in different directions— Why so many then? versus Why so few now?—you would be right to conclude that the history of the apple in America is a curious tale, one that has as much to say about who we are as a people as it does about our favorite pome. You would be right to conclude also that any apple cataloged by Ragan and still being grown today probably has a pretty good story to tell.

Take the 'Ralls Genet', for example. This variety is thought to have originated from cuttings given to Thomas Jefferson by Edmund Charles Genet, French minister to the United States from 1793 to 1794. According to one account, Jefferson passed the cuttings on to Amherst County, Virginia, nurseryman Caleb Ralls, who grafted them and then disseminated the variety throughout Virginia and into the western territories. In time, 'Ralls Genet' emerged as a favorite apple in the Ohio valley because of its late bloom—a characteristic that allows it to weather late-spring frosts unscathed.

But its success was short lived. In the 1920s, commercial orchardists began focusing on growing fewer varieties more efficiently, and as result, many older cultivars fell into disuse. Fortunately, in 1939 'Ralls Genet' got a new lease on life when Japanese breeders dipped into the American gene pool, crossing 'Ralls Genet' with another favorite son, 'Red Delicious'. The resulting apple, christened 'Fuji', was released in 1962 and has gone on to claim a significant share of the commercial market, recently overtaking 'Granny Smith' as the third-most-popular apple in the United States, behind 'Red Delicious' and 'Golden Delicious'. Peter Hatch, director of gardens and grounds at Monticello, the home of Jefferson, sums up well the 'Ralls Genet'-'Fuji' connection. "We like to say that Thomas Jefferson was not only the author of the Declaration of Independence and the father of the University of Virginia, but probably the grandfather of the 'Fuji'."

This is but one story out of thousands hinted at in Ragan's *Nomenclature*. To make sense of them, we must go back to 1607 and Jamestown, Virginia, where North American apple cultivation began. Imagine if you can what it was like to get off a ship and look out over a wild and untamed continent. There were no towns, no stores, very little cleared land on which to grow things—and, except for a few scattered Native American plantings—no cultivated fruit trees, only wild crabapples, mulberries, serviceberries, cherries, plums, pawpaws, and persimmons.

Early Attempts at Fruit Growing

Eventually, the settlers learned how to use these strange fruits. (Taking a bite of an unripe persimmon, Jamestown's Captain John Smith noted, would "draw a man's mouth awrie with much torment.") But in the meantime, the settlers had to get on with the business of feeding their families. And for this they had come prepared with seeds, cuttings, and small plants from the best European stock.

Early attempts at fruit growing were apparently quite successful. In 1629, Smith noted that peaches, apples, apricots, and figs "prosper[ed] exceedingly" in the colony.

In 1642, the first governor of Virginia, William Berkley, cultivated some 1,500 fruit trees at his Green Spring estate, and two years later, he decreed that every planter must, "for every 500 acres granted him ... enclose and fence a quarter-acre of ground near his dwelling house for orchards and gardens."

By 1686, the status of horticulture in Virginia was such that William Fitzhugh of Westmoreland County, describing his plantation in a letter, mentions "a large orchard of about 2,500 apple trees, most grafted, well fenced with a locust fence." And by the close of the century, there were few plantations in Virginia without an orchard—some boasted as many as 10,000 trees.

This rather amazing transplantation of European fruits occurred all up and down the eastern seaboard. But it was not a seamless transition. Many of the grafted fruit trees brought from Europe proved unsuited to the climate of the New World. Harsh winters, late-spring frosts (virtually unknown in England), and summer heat and humidity killed some trees outright and kept others from thriving. Some did take hold, though, and a few of these Old World sorts—varieties like the 'May Duke' cherry, the 'Calville Blanc d'Hiver' apple, and the 'Green Gage' plum—live on today in the orchards of antique fruit collectors and connoisseurs.

Seed-Grown Fruit Trees

It was the seeds from the introduced varieties, more than the varieties themselves, that would spawn a revolution of new American cultivars. Seeds from fruit trees often produce haphazard results. Apple seeds, in particular, are notoriously variable, yielding seedlings, or pippins, that bear often only a glancing resemblance to the parent tree. This tendency, known to botanists as heterozygosity, allowed the apple, by sheer force of numbers, to make itself at home in the New World.

That is the positive side of apple variability. The negative side is that most apple trees grown from seed produce fruit of only passable (or inferior) quality—the pomological equivalent of a mongrel dog, known to apple aficionados as a spitter. Why the settlers would choose to grow seedlings rather than grafting proven varieties—that is, joining cuttings, called scions, to rooted plants, called rootstocks—may seem a mystery. But think again of that fellow who has just come ashore at Jamestown. This man will soon be granted a tract of land that is unthinkably vast by European standards: perhaps a hundred acres, perhaps five hundred. He will have to clear the land by hand

Thomas Jefferson's terraced kitchen garden at Monticello, his Virginia estate, functioned as an experimental laboratory. Among many other crops, apple varieties were nurtured and evaluated for their adaptability to the local climate.

In the mid-1780s, Thomas Jefferson boasted in a letter from Paris to the Reverend James Madison, "They have no apples here to compare with our Newtown pippin."

and get his crops planted—all the while keeping an eye out for members of the indigenous population who don't especially like what he's up to.

Even if this man knows how to graft fruit trees, he has little time to do it. (Furthermore, until about 1800, grafting was generally distrusted anyway. It was thought that grafted stock declined in vigor over time.) And considering the amount of land he intends to convert to orchard, grafted stock is really out of the question. What he needs most are trees that can be propagated cheaply and without a lot of effort. Seedlings are the perfect solution.

Besides that, the chief purpose of the colonial fruit garden was not to grow fruit for the table, but rather to secure a supply of "most excellent and comfortable drinks"—cider from apples, perry from pears, mobby and brandy from peaches. In 1676, Thomas Glover, visiting from England, noted "fair and large orchards" in the New World, "bearing all sorts of English apples ... of which they make great store of cider." Virginian William Fitzhugh allowed that the cider produced from his 2,500 trees was worth as much as 15,000 pounds of tobacco. Since good cider can be made from almost any kind of apple, seedling trees were an ingenious solution for the colonial planter.

Over time, the orchards would serve as vast trial plots for the improvement of imported Old World stocks; occasionally, an apple with unusual and desirable characteristics would arise. This new apple might be rather large, or highly colored, or exceptionally early, or prolific; maybe it kept like a cobblestone or made an exquisite apple pie; maybe it was just the best apple you'd ever tasted. Eventually, the farmer who planted the tree would graft new starts, and this formerly unknown seedling

Johnny Appleseed: Apple Entrepreneur

TIM HENSLEY

John Chapman, better known as Johnny Appleseed, is one of the most enduring American legends. Every year, schoolchildren learn how Johnny befriended a wolf, slept in a hollow log, and wore his dinner pot as a hat. But while these peculiarities make for a good story, they hardly capture the essence of this enigmatic man.

A disciple of Emanuel Swedenborg, the Swedish scientist, philosopher, and theologian, Chapman spread good seeds and a new take on the kingdom of heaven, trekking barefoot in a sackcloth shirt through Pennsylvania, Ohio, and Indiana during the first half of the 19th century. Chapman started his first nursery near Fort Pitt, Pennsylvania, with seeds collected from the cider mills of local farmers. When the frontier moved west, the story goes, Chapman pulled up stakes, gave his farm to a poor woman with children, and headed down the Ohio River in a kind of catamaran made from two hollowed-out logs that were lashed together, one filled with a cargo of precious seeds. The resourceful Massachusetts native scouted routes along which pioneers would most likely settle. He planted apple seedlings on land along these routes, which he willingly dug up and sold—or gave—to arriving settlers. By the 1830s, Chapman owned a string of nurseries that spread from western Pennsylvania across Ohio and into Indiana. He died in 1845 owning 1,200 acres of land.

One of his biographers writes that Chapman "had the thick bark of queerness on him"—and few would disagree. But without this rough covering, "Johnny Appleseed" and other pioneers like him might never have tamed the frontier, sowing it with the seeds of familiar, Old World plants. Chapman's nurseries no doubt produced many valuable new apples. Perhaps a few even made it into W.H. Ragan's USDA Bulletin No. 56, *Nomenclature of the Apple*, the essential reference for apple lovers, which in 1905 cataloged around 17,000 apples.

Apple trees grown from seed, such as those propagated by Johnny Appleseed, gave rise to varieties that were uniquely adapted to the growing conditions in North America. 'Winter Banana' appeared in Indiana around 1836.

Henry David Thoreau held a preference for apples "sour enough to set a squirrel's teeth on edge and make a jay scream."

would join the ranks of new American varieties being passed on to future generations. Thus emerged, for example, the 'Hewes Crab', possibly a cross of an apple of European origin and a native crabapple. In pressing the juice-filled 'Hewes Crab' for cider, wrote Philadelphia farmer Henry Wynkoop in 1814, "the liquor flows from the pumice as water from a sponge."

In time, so many new American apples came to the fore—varieties like 'Father Abraham', 'Monstrous Pippin', 'Roxbury Russet', and 'Maiden's Blush'—that European transplants were soon displaced. In the mid-1780s, Thomas Jefferson boasted in a letter from Paris to the Reverend James Madison, "They have no apples here to compare with our Newtown pippin."

The first American text on pomology, the science of fruit cultivation, was published in 1815 by William Cox. *A View of the Cultivation of Fruit Trees* described "one hundred ... of the most estimable apples cultivated in our country"—most of them American varieties as distinct from the Old World stock as the Americans themselves. These trees would be carried by the settlers across the Appalachian Mountains and into the western frontier, where seedling orchards would again be planted, and yet another generation of new cultivars would emerge.

"It is remarkable how closely the history of the Apple-tree is connected with that of man," wrote Henry David Thoreau in 1862. Of course, Thoreau ate his apples to the beat of a different drummer, lamenting the passage of seedling cider orchards and holding a preference for apples "sour enough to set a squirrel's teeth on edge and make a jay scream." He disavowed faith in the "selected lists of pomological gentle-men." "Their 'Favorites' and 'Nonsuches' and 'Seek-no-farthers'," he wrote, "com-monly turn out very tame and forgettable. They are eaten with comparatively little zest, and have no real tang nor smack to them."

But where Thoreau looked to the wild for sustenance, many Europeans came to prefer the new American sorts. In fact, all during the 19th century, Virginia's Albemarle County enjoyed a lucrative trade exporting the 'Newtown Pippin'. Andrew Stevenson, the American minister to the court of St. James's, was so enthu-siastic about America's "best apple" that he had two barrels of the 'Newtown Pippin' shipped to England in 1838 and gave them to the new queen, Victoria, who was so impressed by his graciousness (and the apple's fine flavor) that she lifted an English tax on imported apples. By 1898, 'Newtown Pippin' was commanding a price at the Liverpool market three times that of any other American apple.

This passion for fine fruit was one of the hallmarks of the 19th century. Andrew Jackson Downing's 1869 *Fruits and Fruit Trees of America* describes nearly 2,000 apples, pears, peaches, plums, and a host of lesser-known fruits—most of American origin. His work is awe inspiring for the number of varieties it describes. When you read the careful descriptions of apples like 'Catface' ("from Kentucky, fruit large, con-ical, truncated"), 'King Tom' ("a crooked, twisting, tangled grower"), 'Summer Pound Royal' ("now pretty widely disseminated in some parts of Michigan, Ohio, and in the South and West"), and 'Sweet Bellflower' ("slightly ribbed, greenish yel-low, with a few brown dots"), you realize just how serious 19th-century gardeners were about growing their own fruit.

The Arrival of Mass-Market Apples

The golden age of American pomology came to an abrupt end in the early 20th cen-tury. Inexpensive railway shipping and mechanical refrigeration enabled orchards to distribute apples year-round. Home orcharding declined as suburbs emerged. Large concerns in the West forced many smaller orchards in the East out of business. And when those quintessential mass-market apples, the patented and inoffensively sweet 'Red Delicious' and 'Golden Delicious', took hold in the early 1920s, many highly fla-vored heirlooms were effectively cut out of the commercial trade.

How two such average apples could displace a host of fine cultivars is a story in itself. Both were introduced by Stark Bro's Nursery, of Louisiana, Missouri. 'Red Delicious', a chance seedling from Iowa, turned out to be amazingly productive in a variety of soils, a characteristic that Stark Bro's touted with great effect. 'Golden Delicious' was discovered by Paul Stark on a hillside farm in Odessa, West Virginia. As the story goes, Stark traveled 1,000 miles by train and 20 miles on horseback to see for himself the apple that a farmer, Anderson Mullins, had sent him samples of two years running. Stark reported that when he first surveyed Mullins's orchard, he found only a dismal mix of wild seedlings—"miserable runts." But then, as he started to leave, he turned around and "Saw it!: There, looming forth in the midst of leafless, barren trees was one tree with green foliage, that looked as if it had been transplanted from the Garden of Eden. That tree's boughs were bending to the ground beneath a tremendous crop of great, glorious, glowing golden apples."

Before the day was over, Stark had paid $5,000 for the tree, roughly $100,000 in today's economy. He then built a two-story, woven-wire cage around it to deter any would-be propagators. That in itself was enough to make you want a cutting. Little wonder, then, that photographs of the caged tree, with its $5,000 price tag, were prominently displayed in every Stark Bro's catalog for years to come.

One Red, One Green, One Yellow

Today's mass merchandisers aren't nearly so sensational. But given the increasing homogeneity of American culture, and what Peter Hatch calls "our peculiarly suburban alienation from the land," it may be that sensationalism is no longer needed to promote an average apple. "One of the weaknesses of consumers," wrote George Holmes in the *United States Department of Agriculture Yearbook, 1904*, "is an admiration for foods that are polished or have a gloss, and this nickel-plate fancy plays some queer pranks with foods."

If Holmes were writing today, his comments would no doubt be much the same. Mass merchandisers now view apple varieties in terms of color, disease resistance, shelf life, and their ability to ship long distances without bruising. Grocery stores often stock only one red, one green, and one yellow variety, which usually means 'Red Delicious', 'Golden Delicious', and 'Granny Smith'. And as any consumer knows, those big, beautiful, and perfect-looking apples often taste like sweetened sawdust.

Still, the apple remains big business in this country today: About 7,500 commercial apple producers in 36 states harvest 48,000 tons of fruit, second in production only to China. The average American consumes some 16 pounds of apples each year, making the apple the nation's most popular fruit after the banana.

How long the apple will retain this status is open to debate. Some breeders worry

Selected for consistently good looks and tolerance for repeated shipping and handling, today's shiny supermarket apples may be larger and prettier than some older varieties. However, these heirlooms more than make up in intense flavor what they may lack in cosmetic appeal.

that the exclusive use of grafted trees in American orchards is a prescription for disaster, since cloned trees, cut off from the broader *Malus* gene pool, are less able to adapt to increasing insect and disease pressure. Others breeders are more optimistic and have initiated breeding programs that cross and back-cross commercially viable apples (including some heirlooms, which are enjoying an increasing popularity today) with crabapples and other *Malus* species in hopes that once again, new, hardier, and tastier varieties will emerge from the American soil, each to play its own unique role in the curious tale that is the history of the apple in America.

Antique Apples: A Guide for Eaters and Growers

Ian A. Merwin

Most antique or heirloom apples are distant cousins to the commercial varieties available on supermarket shelves today. While modern varieties such as 'Red Delicious' have been selected for their consistent appearance, cosmetic appeal, and tolerance of long shipping and repeated handling, antique varieties were often selected for their cider-making quality ('Golden Russet'), their retention of flavor and firmness without refrigeration ('Winesap' and 'Baldwin'), or their intense and unusual flavor—without regard to external appearance. Until modern growing, storing, and transportation technologies revolutionized apple cultivation in the 1920s, farmers preferred late-ripening, hard apples that remained edible after many months in a cool cellar, were relatively tolerant of pests, and grew vigorously in pasture orchards without fertilizers or weed control. For example, 'Macoun' and 'Northern Spy' are well suited to cool-climate regions of the Northeast and can tolerate the cold winters of that region. Today's home fruit growers may appreciate these same traits—but they must be prepared for apples that can be rather rough in appearance, require a few months in the cellar to mellow and attain their characteristic flavors, and produce a crop only every few years (a good pest-avoidance strategy for the tree). They also have to contend with trees that are extremely vigorous and quickly outgrow their limited space in the backyard, unless they are grown on one of several dwarfing rootstocks

Eating and growing antique apple varieties are the best ways to ensure their survival. Home orchardists will appreciate their disease and pest resistance but should be prepared for trees that produce a crop only every other year.

available today. But home growers will be rewarded for all their troubles with a tasty crop that offers varied and unusual fruit flavors and textures, excellent cider making or cooking attributes, and a unique eating experience. 'Roxbury Russet', for example, provides an unusual tart, nutty flavor and makes excellent pie and cider too. 'Keepsake' remains wonderfully crisp and juicy for many months and has a delicate anise flavor that belies its rustic exterior.

Seeking out antique apples can become real detective work. Varieties often have a slew of synonyms or local names—'Lady Apple', for example, has also been called at various times and places 'Lady's Finger,' 'Petit Api', 'Pomme d'Api', 'Pomme Rose', 'Christmas Apple', 'Lady Sweet', and dozens of other names. 'Fameuse' is also called 'Snow Apple', 'Snow Chimney', 'Chimney Apple', 'Red American', 'Royal Snow', and 'Chimney Point'. Synonyms for 'Baldwin' include 'Butter Apple', 'Woodpecker' or 'Pecker', 'Flech', and 'Steel's Red Winter'. Growers either assigned these various names in good faith to what they thought were newly discovered apples, or enterprising farmers and nursery operators concocted the names as part of their marketing strategies. Whatever the motives behind the array of names antique apples accrued, the resulting confusion has made it difficult to say with certainty which apple is which.

Pomologists in North America and Europe have gathered and preserved samples of almost 5,000 presumably different varieties of apples by placing seeds and/or vegetative cuttings in major germplasm repositories in Geneva, New York; Angers, France; Villaviciosa, Spain; and East Malling, England. (Detailed descriptions and information about the national apple collection in Geneva is available online at www.ars-grin.gov/gen/applesmain.html.) The definitive scientific identification and genetic characterization of each variety in these collections were until recently somewhat suspect, but they

Unlike 'Rome Beauty', which has been going strong since 1846, other old North American apple varieties may have been lost or survive only in the germplasm repository in Geneva, New York.

Unusual and intense flavor, superior cider-making qualities, and good storage potential without refrigeration would assure an apple variety a place in a 19th-century nursery catalog—and in the orchard of a 21st-century apple aficionado.

HAVE AN APPLE?

WITH COMPLIMENTS OF

GREEN'S NURSERY COMPANY, Rochester, N. Y.

Fall of 1898.

October and November is the time to plant trees, vines, etc. Send us your order now.

Copyright 1898 by Green's Nursery Co.

have become considerably more precise thanks to new technologies such as DNA fingerprinting. This technique has already revealed some duplications that have resulted from apple varieties with multiple names. Even so, there is really no way to know what proportion of the truly unique apple varieties, or genotypes, are included in the world's apple germplasm collections and conserved for posterity, and how many have been lost forever.

Save Antique Apples by Growing Them

The best way to ensure the survival of antique apples is to grow them in small plantings in diverse conditions around the world. These plantings provide insurance against possible disease introductions or weather events that could strike the large germplasm collections described above. Home and small-scale commercial orchardists are the ideal agents to carry out this mission. Many home orchardists have become interested in old varieties, both for personal enjoyment and as a way to help conserve the apple's genetic heritage. No matter where you live, you are likely to find from a few to dozens of antique apples suited to your region. You'll find many of these described in "60 Great Apples," starting on page 29. You'll also find an introduction to the basics of apple growing, starting on page 88. An excellent source of information for gardeners interested in growing antique varieties is the *Fruit, Berry and Nut Inventory*, by Kent Whealy and Joanne Thuente. It is one of several compilations of antique fruit and vegetable varieties supported by the Seed Savers Exchange, in Decorah, Iowa. It includes a comprehensive listing and brief descrip-

Unusual antique apple varieties are often for sale at farmers' markets, shown above, or at pick-your-own orchards, as many small-scale farmers specialize in old varieties. If you have the time and inclination, you can also try your hand at growing time-tested varieties that thrive in your area.

tions of the climate zones and pest susceptibility for the 1,513 apple varieties currently available as grafted trees from commercial nurseries in North America. It has similar information about many other fruit and nut crops. Several nurseries around the United States and Canada now specialize in young trees of antique apple varieties. These are listed on page 110.

Save Them by Eating Them

If you don't have the space, time, or desire to grow antique apples in your garden, you can still enjoy their distinctive flavors and tree-ripened succulence. You are likely to find a few local varieties at nearby farmers' markets or at pick-your-own orchards in your area, and many small-scale farmers around the country now specialize in antique varieties. A good place to start searching for orchards near you is the Orchard Trail, which can be found on the *Apple Journal* website (http://www.applejournal.com/trail.htm). This site lists orchards and their contact information throughout the United States, Canada, and several other countries. If your area lacks orchards or farmers' markets, you can still sample these fruits by ordering antique apples online from growers around the country. A few of these mail-order orchards are listed on page 110. Keep in mind that the shipping costs can be substantial and that ripened fruit may suffer during transit.

Save Them by Finding Them

Trees of antique varieties sometimes survive, lost and neglected, in old fields and forests, abandoned homesteads, and even suburban backyards. For this reason devotees are always on the lookout for old apple trees with unusual fruits. It is not easy to identify a tree that hasn't been pruned or protected from pests. To determine a tree's identity, apple experts use a number of methods. Among them are a close examination of some basic attributes:

- healthy fruit, including lengthwise and crosswise sections, patterns of stripes and russeting (brownish roughened patches of skin), red or orange blush and underlying green, white or yellow skin color of ripe fruit
- bark patterns
- presence or absence of fuzziness (pubescence) on leaves and young stems
- the typical vigor of the tree

In some regions, local commercial growers or curators at botanical gardens and germplasm repositories may be able to identify varieties. Local pick-your-own orchards that specialize in antique apples are another good place to get information. You can browse their plantings looking for apples similar to your own, or take in a few samples of clean, sound fruit to see if they can be identified. If there are master gardeners or cooperative extension agents in your county, they may know of local horticulturists who can identify antique or unusual apple varieties.

In any case, well-formed edible apples that are free of "worms" and rots are essential for identification purposes. Sampling a few young twigs and healthy leaves can also be helpful, as bark and leaf characteristics are useful traits for identification. Even when you can't positively identify a rare or antique apple tree, by grafting a few buds of a tasty variety

Originally from northern France, where it was first recorded in 1535, 'Summer Rambo' was growing in colonial America as early as 1767.

Left: 'Stayman', a chance seedling of 'Winesap' discovered on a Kansas farm in the mid-1800s, quickly gained popularity.

Right: 'Grimes Golden' originated in West Virginia in 1804, near a cider mill and farm established by John Chapman, better known as Johnny Appleseed.

onto another tree or a rootstock (see page 92), you can still grow and enjoy it as your own special mystery apple.

Another wonderful resource for serious antique apple research is *The Apples of New York*, published by S.A. Beach in 1905, which is out of print, but available at university and other specialized libraries. The two-volume set contains extensive descriptions and illustrations of apples cultivated in the eastern United States during the late 1800s—an era when thousands of small farms included orchards of local varieties that are no longer grown commercially. As yet there is no illustrated Web-based apple identification key; a tool like this would greatly facilitate the characterization and conservation of antique apples.

Classic Delicacies: Cider and Pie

The Makings of a Good Cider

Ian A. Merwin

For at least 2,000 years, humans have been making apple cider wherever they could grow the fruit. In America between 1650 and 1850, almost every Yankee farmer had a basement full of cider barrels, and hard cider was on the table for each meal. By the mid-19th century, however, cider was being supplanted by beer, and cider making was eventually singled out for suppression by the temperance movement. In most apple-growing regions of the world today, the term cider means a beverage made from the juice of milled apples that has been collected in large barrels and fermented with yeast, like grape wines. Only in North America is fresh or sweet cider a popular drink. Elsewhere, fresh cider is either processed into apple juice, fermented to make hard cider, or fermented and then distilled and blended to make apple brandy, applejack, or eau-de-vie.

Apple juice averages about 13 percent sugar, which produces a naturally fermented cider with around 6 percent alcohol by volume. Fermentation begins within a few days in a barrel of cider at cellar temperatures, around 55°F, and is completed in several months. Fermentation in an environment that is somewhat cooler than typical room temperature often improves the flavor of cider. If it is kept in an airtight container with a suitable "airlock" that permits carbon dioxide (produced by yeast as it converts sugar into ethanol) to escape but prevents oxygen from entering, hard cider will keep for a year or more; after that its flavor does not improve much. In the presence of oxygen, bacteria will eventually convert hard cider into a vinegar that has many culinary purposes.

In most states it is legal to produce small quantities (up to a few hundred gallons annually) of beer, wine, or hard cider for personal consumption, and the basic equipment for home fermentation is readily available at beer or wine-making supply stores.

The best ciders are made from a blend of many varieties: some with lots of acidity, others high in sugar, and some that impart desirable flavors and aromatic qualities to the cider. Tart apples such as 'Baldwin', 'Calville Blanc', 'Empire', 'Esopus Spitzenberg', 'Golden Russet', 'GoldRush', 'Idared', 'Liberty', 'McIntosh', 'Mutsu', 'Newtown Pippin', 'Northern Spy', 'Roxbury Russet', and 'Winesap' are excellent *sharps* for cider blends. Apples that are typically high in sugar, such as 'Golden Delicious', 'Fuji', 'Gala', 'Golden Russet', 'GoldRush', 'Jonagold', 'Red Delicious', and many others are wonderful *sweets*. Apple varieties with astringent tannins impart flavors other than sweet and tart, adding complexity, a long finish, and a rich "mouthfeel" to sweet or hard ciders. These apples are known in Europe as *bittersweets* if they are high in tannins and sugars, or *bittertarts* if they have both acidity and tannins. A few of the dessert and culinary apples included in the encyclopedia—'Golden Russet', 'Northern Spy', and 'Liberty'—add significant amounts of tannins and other unique flavors to cider blends. Some crabapples grown as ornamental trees produce

A mill, such as this hand-cranked model, plus a variety of flavorful apples is all that's needed to make delicious cider, to be enjoyed fresh, processed into juice, or fermented to make hard cider.

fruit high in tannins and acidity and can be blended with sweet and tart apples to make a good hard cider.

High-quality European-style fermented ciders include about 20 percent of bittersweet varieties such as 'Tremletts Bitter', 'Hereford Redstreak' and 'Somerset Redstreak', 'Dabinett', 'Chisel Jersey', 'Kingston Black', 'Ellis Bitter', 'Binet Rouge', or 'Medaille D'Or'. Trees of these varieties are available from several nurseries specializing in antique apples. They can be grown successfully in Zones 5 to 7 but do best in cooler regions with long, mild summers. These will provide plenty of tannins in a cider blend.

Elements of a Perfect Apple Pie
Tom Burford

The prize-winning apple pie marries an exemplary crust with tree-ripened apples that contribute acid, tannin, sugar, and flavor. A bad crust with the best apples makes a fair pie and a good crust with fair apples makes a good pie, but a good crust with great apples makes an excellent and memorable pie. Remember that the flavor of the apples and the crust should dominate the pie, not spices, excessive sugar, or lemon juice.

In colonial America, 'Rhode Island Greening' in New England and 'Winesap' and 'Stayman' in the Mid-Atlantic states were the choices for pie making, equivalent to

Experimentation is the road to one's own signature apple pie.

The Perfect Apple Pie

Here is a basic apple pie recipe from the *Home Comfort* cookbook that my grand-parents received with the purchase of a super-fancy wood-burning cookstove in the early 1930s. Characteristic of many recipes of the time, it assumes a certain level of cooking and baking skill. I've added the baking temperature that works for most apple pies.

MAKING THE CRUST

1$\frac{1}{2}$ cups flour	6 tablespoons shortening (vegetable or lard)
1 teaspoon baking powder	$\frac{1}{4}$ cup cold water
$\frac{1}{2}$ teaspoon salt	

These ingredients will make one two-crust pie.

Sift flour, baking powder, and salt together. Cut in cold shortening with a dough blender until it resembles coarse meal. Add cold water slowly until the dough is moist enough to stick together but not so sticky it clings to hands or bowl. You may need one or two more tablespoons of cold water, depending on the kind of flour. Divide the dough in half and chill for about an hour; then put each half on a lightly floured board and roll out with light outward motions until it is $\frac{1}{4}$-inch thick. Put one half in a pie pan, pat down, and trim off the surplus. Press down the edges with a fork or finger. Prick the bottom with a fork a few times. Bake in a hot oven (400°F) until slightly browned.

ASSEMBLING THE APPLE PIE

6 to 8 medium-sized apples	$\frac{1}{8}$ teaspoon salt
$\frac{1}{2}$ to $\frac{2}{3}$ cup white or brown sugar	1 to 1$\frac{1}{4}$ tablespoons cornstarch
$\frac{1}{2}$ teaspoon cinnamon	1$\frac{1}{2}$ tablespoons butter
$\frac{1}{8}$ teaspoon nutmeg	

Peel, core, and thinly slice the apples. Sift the sugar, cornstarch, spices, and salt over the apples and stir gently until they are well coated. Place the apples in layers in the half-baked pie shell, dotting each layer with bits of butter. If the apples are dry, add 2 tablespoons of water or cream. Cover with the pricked upper crust and bake in a hot oven (400°F) until done, about 30 or 40 minutes.

Apples for Pies

The apples in this chart have been divided into three groups based on the balance of acid, tannin, and sugar they contain. **Acid-tannin** varieties require blending with sugar or acid-tannin-sugar varieties. **Acid-tannin-sugar** varieties alone make a good pie. **Sugar** varieties need acid and tannin from apples in the other columns.

ACID-TANNIN VARIETIES	ACID-TANNIN-SUGAR VARIETIES	SUGAR VARIETIES
'Arkansas Black'	'Golden Russet'	'Gala'
'Baldwin'	'Goldrush'	'Golden Delicious'
'Cortland'	'Idared'	'Grimes Golden'
'Duchess of Oldenburg'	'McIntosh'	'Red Delicious'
'Granny Smith'	'Newtown Pippin'	
'Gravenstein'	'Northern Spy'	
'Jonathan'	'Ralls Genet'	
'Lodi'	'Razor Russet'	
'Lowland Raspberry'	'Roxbury Russet'	
'Mammoth Blacktwig'	'Smokehouse'	
'Red Astrachan'	'Spartan'	
'Rhode Island Greening'	'York'	
'Stayman'		
'Winesap'		
'Yellow Transparent'		

today's 'Granny Smith'. The classic pie maker of England was 'Bramley's Seedling', which contains an extraordinary 1 percent acid, one of the highest of all apple varieties. Except from specialty orchards, it is seldom available in North America or England but is worth seeking out.

If these classic pie apples are not available, one or two sweet varieties blended with one or two tart (acid-tannin) varieties from the chart above will make hundreds of taste combinations. Part of the success in making a memorable pie is variety selection and the quality of these varieties.

60 Great Apples

On the following pages you will find portraits of 60 scrumptious apple varieties commonly grown in North America, organized in alphabetical order. Each entry provides a detailed description of the apple's characteristic features, its flavor and aroma, and the best culinary uses. Also included is information on when each variety is harvested and how long it keeps.

For home growers, the articles also provide specific growing tips for each variety. Unless otherwise noted, varieties are hardy in Zones 4 to 8. A map of the USDA hardiness zones appears on page 115. For more in-depth information on apple culture in general, please refer to "The ABCs of Growing Apples at Home," starting on page 88.

The encyclopedia was written by Tom Burford (TB), Ian A. Merwin (IM), Curt Rom (CR), and Ted Swensen (TS).

A tart-sweet early apple that's crisp and juicy, 'Akane' is wonderful for fresh eating, baking, and sauce making.

'Akane'

'Akane', a bright red, round apple, is one of the better-tasting early varieties, with the tart-sweet flavor of its parent 'Jonathan'. It is the result of a cross between 'Jonathan' and 'Worcester Pearmain' at the Tohoku Agricultural Experiment Station, in Japan, and was introduced in the United States in 1970. The small to medium-sized apple has thin skin and white, crisp, juicy flesh, with a slight hint of strawberry flavor. It is also called 'Prime Red', 'Tokyo Rose', and, in France, 'Primrouge'.

CULINARY USES 'Akane' is great for fresh eating. The fruit maintains its shape and flavor when baked and makes a flavorful pink sauce when cooked with peels and strained; pie slices keep their shape. It is also a great apple for drying. The fruit does not keep well after harvest, so use promptly.

HARVEST TIME Late August to early September. This apple hangs well on the tree when ripe, which allows harvesting over an extended period of time.

REGIONS WHERE GROWN Pacific Northwest, Pennsylvania, warmer regions of southern Canada.

GROWING TIPS 'Akane' is a moderately vigorous variety. On a dwarfing rootstock like M.9, it grows 8 to 12 feet tall and requires staking and irrigation; on M.26 dwarfing rootstock, 'Akane' reaches 12 to 16 feet tall and requires staking. Spread limbs on young trees to 45- to 60-degree angles for good fruiting. 'Akane' bears a crop annually, setting fruit heavily even with adverse weather during pollination. It requires a pollinator such as 'Cortland' or 'Grimes Golden'. The fruit tends to be small, so thin to one apple per spur (within 40 days of petal fall) to increase fruit size. It is moderately resistant to scab, mildew, and fire blight.

—TS

'Arkansas Black'

In the early 20th century, 'Arkansas Black' enjoyed a modicum of popularity for three distinct qualities: It is harvested late; it is hard, which allowed growers to barrel it for shipping; and it lasts a long time in storage—until late winter in an icehouse. Its attractive appearance also gained it a first-place commendation at the 1900 International Exposition in Paris. But it is probably more popular today as an antique apple than it was a century ago as a commercial crop. The attractive, glossy fruits are round to somewhat conical in cooler regions, medium sized, and dark purple-red or "black" with some white spotting. In humid regions, russet streaks often emanate from the stem end of the fruit. The flesh is a yellow to cream color and very firm or even hard, with a coarse, almost woody texture. The apple has a mild but balanced flavor, more sweet than acidic. This apple was found on a farm near Bentonville, Arkansas, in 1870 and is thought to be a 'Winesap' seedling.

CULINARY USES 'Arkansas Black' can be enjoyed fresh as a dessert apple, though it is very hard. It may be better cooked, dried, used in sauce, fried, or in a cider blend. Fruits can be stored for several months. When left to become overripe on the tree or in storage, they will soften and become mealy, and develop a very greasy surface.

Mild and sweet but also rather hard, 'Arkansas Black' is better suited to cooking and cider making than fresh eating. It is harvested late and keeps well in storage.

HARVEST TIME Late fall.

REGIONS WHERE GROWN The South through the lower Midwest.

GROWING TIPS This moderately vigorous, spreading tree bears fruit on both spurs and short shoots. Prune carefully every year to remove some older wood and some fruiting spurs. Thin fruit to improve fruit size. This variety blooms late, often avoiding spring frosts. It is very tolerant of summer heat and can be grown in any region with a sufficiently long season to allow its ripening late in the fall (it requires at least 150 frost-free days after bloom). Spur forms of the tree (which are naturally occurring mutations) are very compact, tend to produce smaller fruit, and grow poorly; standard forms grafted to dwarfing rootstocks are preferred. 'Arkansas Black' is resistant to cedar-apple rust and fire blight and somewhat resistant to some insects, especially mites. It is susceptible to apple scab and surface infections of sooty blotch and flyspeck.

—CR

'Ashmead's Kernel'

'Ashmead's Kernel' is a juicy, aromatic apple with a sharp flavor that's both acidic and sweet; the crisp yellowish flesh is tinged green. Because of its pronounced flavor, some say that it "is not an apple for sissies," and its potato-like appearance has earned it the moniker "that ugly apple." Fruits are medium sized, flattish to round, sometimes conical or lopsided; the dry skin is russeted a golden brown with an orange or reddish bronze cheek. Named after a physician from Gloucester, England, who raised this variety in about 1700, it is thought to be a seedling of 'Nonpareil', another highly flavored variety. It is now a popular tree propagated in specialty nurseries. 'Ashmead's Kernel', 'Roxbury Russet', and 'Golden Russet' are all gaining a following and appearing more frequently in organic food and farmers' markets.

CULINARY USES Several weeks of storage enhance the memorable flavor of 'Ashmead's Kernel'—the apple's high acid content takes time to balance with its sugar. This classic English dessert fruit is also suitable for cooking and pie making. It can be stored for three to four months.

HARVEST TIME Late September to early October.

REGIONS WHERE GROWN All apple-growing regions.

GROWING TIPS 'Ashmead's Kernel' sets fruit in clusters on short spurs, so shorten the laterals back to three or four buds during late-winter pruning to encourage spur formation. Thin the fruit annually to produce a good crop every year. Remove some of the tree's straggly growth each year to improve air circulation and sunlight penetration, which helps reduce fungal activity. Despite your best efforts, fruit production can be erratic, and fruit size diminishes as the tree ages. 'Ashmead's Kernel' is resistant to powdery mildew and somewhat resistant to scab.

—*TB*

'Baldwin'

The yellowish-white flesh of 'Baldwin' is crisp, tender, and moderately acidic. It has a distinctive flavor actually called the "Baldwin taste." Fruits are large and roundish, narrowing just a little toward the blossom end. The skin is yellow with crimson stripes that nearly cover the apple on the sun-exposed side. The surface is spattered with white, star-shaped flecks. Until 1934, 'Baldwin' was widely grown in the Northeast, but temperatures that winter reached minus 40°F, devastating 'Baldwin' orchards. 'McIntosh', which originated in Canada and bears a heavy crop annually, was chosen to replace it. An 1847 publica-

'Ashmead's Kernel' tastes best after several weeks in storage—the apple's acid content takes time to balance with its sugar.

Moderately acidic with a distinctive taste actually named after the variety, 'Baldwin' was widely grown in the Northeast until 1934, when brutally cold winter temperatures devastated orchards.

tion, *The Horticulturist and Journal of Rural Art and Rural Taste,* noted that 'Baldwin', which was discovered about 1750, originated near Boston: "The original tree grew on the farm of Mr. Butters and was known for a time as the 'Butters' apple. Woodpeckers frequented this tree, and Mr. Butters called it the 'Woodpecker' apple, which was soon abbreviated to the 'Pecker' apple." 'Baldwin' is also called 'Flech' and 'Steel's Red Winter'.

CULINARY USES Delicious for dessert and pies. Its high sugar content also makes 'Baldwin' valuable for cider production. It stores well for a number of months.

HARVEST TIME Late September in the warmer zones and October elsewhere.

REGIONS WHERE GROWN 'Baldwin' produces the highest-quality fruit in New England, but it also does well at higher elevations in the mountains regions of Maryland, Virginia, and North Carolina.

GROWING TIPS The tree is slow to begin bearing and is biennial, bearing a heavy crop one year and a light crop the next. 'Baldwin' is also pollen sterile and must have a pollinator, like 'Golden Delicious' or a crabapple, to set a full crop of fruit. The thick skin of 'Baldwin' protects it from bruising and possibly some insect damage, but it is subject to scab infection and 'Baldwin' spot, a physiological condition of brown flecks in the flesh just under the skin that does not affect the taste but will shorten the otherwise long storage. It is very resistant to cedar-apple rust. 'Baldwin' is hardy in Zones 4 to 6. In Zone 7, it succeeds only when planted in the mountains above 1,500 feet in elevation.

—*TB*

'Belle de Boskoop'

A firm, crisp, tangy or tart, highly aromatic juicy apple, 'Belle de Boskoop' has richly flavored creamy-white, rather coarse flesh. The fruits are medium to large and round to conical. The skin is rough, dull, and russeted. In the Pacific Northwest, the skin is often almost completely covered with bright red, obscuring the stripes of a deeper dark red blush. Elsewhere, the skin is deep yellow or greenish yellow. 'Belle de Boskoop' is named after the small community of Boskoop, Holland, where it was discovered in 1856 by K.J.W. Ottolander. Apparently an offspring of 'Reinette de Montfort', it's also called 'Schone van Boskoop', 'Boskoop', 'Gold Reinette', 'Goudrent', 'Monstrous Reinette', and many other names.

CULINARY USES 'Belle de Boskoop' is very high in vitamin C and outstanding as a dessert fruit; it is tart but mellows with age. When cooked or baked, it keeps its shape, and it makes a thick, well-flavored, golden puree that's quite brisk and needs hardly any sugar. It is also good for cider. The fruit keeps well and sweetens in storage.

HARVEST TIME October.

REGIONS WHERE GROWN Suitable for cool and humid regions such as the Pacific Northwest

GROWING TIPS The tree is moderately vigorous with long, somewhat stout, spreading open limbs and short and stocky twigs with fruit borne on spurs. 'Belle de Boskoop' has attractive blossoms. As it is a triploid variety with sterile pollen, you need at least two other trees for proper pollination. They will pollinate the triploid and each other. 'Empire', 'Fireside', and 'Keepsake' work well. A dwarfing rootstock, such as M.9 or M.26, will control tree size. This apple is moderately resistant to scab, resistant to canker, and very resistant to fire blight.

—TS

'Bramley's Seedling'

American horticulturist Norman Taylor labeled 'Bramley's Seedling' "the greatest cooking apple of the century" (the 20th), and in the United Kingdom it is the apple most favored for pies. Its firm, greenish-yellow skin has broad, broken brown and red stripes and is smooth, shiny, and greasy when the fruit is ripe. The large fruit is somewhat blocky and irregularly shaped with firm, yellowish-white, juicy flesh that has a sharply acidic flavor unless the apple is picked when completely ripe. 'Bramley's Seedling' was named after the Nottinghamshire butcher in whose garden it was growing in the mid-19th century. It is also called 'Bramley', 'Bramley's Sämling', and 'Triomphe de Kiel'.

A tart apple that mellows with age, 'Belle de Boskoop' is outstanding for fresh eating and makes a thick sauce that's brisk and flavorful.

Left: 'Bramley's Seedling' keeps its acidic flavor in cooking, making it a favorite for sauces and pies. Right: 'Brock' resembles its parent 'Golden Delicious' in flavor and aroma.

CULINARY USES 'Bramley's Seedling' cooks to a pale, creamy puree. Its strong acidic flavor remains intact when the apple is cooked and is rarely overwhelmed in sugary or highly spiced recipes.

HARVEST TIME Late October.

REGIONS WHERE GROWN Pacific Northwest, Midwest from Nebraska and central Oklahoma up to southern Maine.

GROWING TIPS This vigorously growing tree has large leathery leaves and bright pink blossoms. Control its size by growing it on a dwarfing rootstock (M.9 to M.26). To protect it from spring frosts, hang outdoor Christmas lights with large bulbs in the tree. As a triploid this tree produces sterile pollen. To ensure proper pollination, combine it with two other varieties: 'Katy', 'Lord Lambourne', or 'Pink Pearl' are good choices. The fruits do not hang well if the tree sets too many, so thin them to one fruit per spur or tip. 'Bramley's Seedling' is moderately resistant to scab and mildew; it is prone to bitter pit, a

result of calcium deficiency. It is susceptible to spring frosts and hardy in Zones 4 to 6.

—*TS*

'Brock'

This offspring of a 'McIntosh' and 'Golden Delicious' cross has white to cream-colored, crisp, aromatic, juicy flesh with a good sweet-tart balance. In aroma and flavor it resembles its parent 'Golden Delicious'. The fruit is medium to large with a rusty-red blush over a yellow ground. 'Brock' originated at the University of Maine in 1934 and was named after Henry Brock, an apple grower in Alfred, Maine.

CULINARY USES The fruit's flavor and unusually small core make it good for sauces and pies. Slices of 'Brock' do not oxidize (turn brown), so it is ideal for salads and freezing as slices. Dessert quality has been rated as good or better than 'McIntosh'. 'Brock' stores well in colder areas but holds up for only about a month in warmer areas.

HARVEST TIME Depending on location, mid-September to late October, just after 'Golden Delicious'. The fruit hangs well on the tree when ripe, giving 'Brock' an extended harvest season.

REGIONS WHERE GROWN Pacific Northwest and Maine; warmer parts of southern Canada.

GROWING TIPS 'Brock' is a vigorous and spreading tree with branches that form desirably wide angles; it bears its fruits on spurs. Grow it on a dwarfing rootstock like M.9 or M.26 to control size. In colder areas use a cold-hardy rootstock such as Ottawa 3 or B.9. This tree bears a good crop annually if it is thinned within 40 days of petal fall. 'Brock' is hardy in Zones 4 to 7 but does best in Zone 4, upper Zone 5, and the western part of Zone 7.

—*TS*

'Calville Blanc d'Hiver'

This classic dessert apple of France is of either French or German origin and probably dates to the late 16th century. LeLectier, procurer for Louis XIII at Orleans, noted it in 1627. It was planted in the Gardens of Versailles by Jean-Baptiste de la Quintinie, gardener to Louis XIV, during the installation of the orchard and kitchen garden from 1678 to 1683. The apple is large and flattish to round with prominent uneven ribs terminating in unequal ridges at the base. Its pale green skin develops an orange color and light red dots on the sun-exposed side. Its distinctive appearance made it a frequent subject of Renaissance fruit paintings, and Claude Monet included it in his 1879 still life *Apples and Grapes*. The tart and rich taste is often described as effervescent.

CULINARY USES This is the definitive apple for the classic French apple tart. In the 19th and early 20th centuries it was served with cheeses in Paris sidewalk cafes. Not only is it an excellent dessert apple, but it also makes exceptional cider, and vinegar made from 'Calville Blanc d'Hiver' is highly prized. Its vitamin C content is very high, exceeding that of an orange. When it begins to turn yellow in storage it is ready to eat, and after a month or longer it will reach its maximum flavor.

HARVEST TIME Early October in New England and upper Midwest. Early to late September elsewhere. Pick fruit before the skin becomes yellow.

REGIONS WHERE GROWN Throughout the apple-growing areas of the country it will produce fruit of fair quality, but in New England and the upper Midwest it produces outstanding apples.

GROWING TIPS This vigorous tree with weeping branches needs a sunny location for the fruit to ripen fully and develop their best flavor. It is an annual light to moderate bearer and takes a number of years to produce its highest-quality fruit. If the tree is fed too much nitrogen, the apple skins will be particularly green and the fruit's flavor will be diminished. It is susceptible to scab and very susceptible to powdery mildew. It is hardy in Zones 4 to 7.

—*TB*

'Cox's Orange Pippin'

Its crisp texture and richly aromatic, semitart flavor have made this chance

An excellent dessert apple, 'Calville Blanc d'Hiver' also makes exceptional cider and is the basis of a highly prized vinegar.

seedling, or pippin, the most popular apple in the United Kingdom, and it is much appreciated elsewhere around the world. It is a seedling of 'Ribston Pippin' from England (circa 1825) and the grandparent of 'Gala' and 'Sansa'. The medium-sized fruit has an orange-red blush over a creamy-yellow background, and it is lightly russeted. The apple is not widely available commercially in the United States, but it is much in demand at local farmers' markets and pick-your-own orchards.

CULINARY USES 'Cox's Orange Pippin' is a multipurpose apple good for cooking or cider as well as fresh eating. It keeps well for two to three months in storage.

HARVEST TIME Late September.

REGIONS WHERE GROWN Worldwide but especially in England, New Zealand, and the eastern United States.

GROWING TIPS This moderately vigorous tree prefers fertile soil. The tree comes into production quickly on a dwarfing rootstock and produces a reliable but light crop when adequately thinned. It is quite susceptible to scab and other diseases and prone to cracking and heat stress in hot climates. Although not an easy apple to grow, 'Cox's Orange Pippin' is worth the effort for growers in the Northeast, where it is usually within its climate comfort zone. It attains its full potential in cool climates, Zones 5 to 7.

—IM

'Cripps Pink'

'Cripps Pink' derives its name from its skin's lovely pink to light red blush over a green to yellow undercolor. Fruits are medium sized with a slightly oblong, blocky shape. They are glossy and smooth, but in humid regions they may show some russeting in the stem cavity. When ripe, the fruits are dense, firm to hard, with a high sugar content but a balanced sweet-acid flavor. The flesh has

Richly aromatic and semitart, 'Cox's Orange Pippin' is much in demand at farmers' markets.

High in sugar with a balanced sweet-acid flavor, 'Cripps Pink' is a multipurpose apple that keeps well for several months in storage.

a cream to yellow color and does not readily brown when cut. 'Cripps Pink' was the result of a 'Golden Delicious' and 'Lady Williams' cross by Australian nurseryman John Cripps; it was released in 1973. Fruits that meet specific grade standards for size, color, and quality may also be sold as Pink Lady, a trademarked name for 'Cripps Pink'.

CULINARY USES This multipurpose apple cooks well, preserving its flavor and texture in pies and sauces. It's also an excellent dessert apple. 'Cripps Pink' remains firm and flavorful for several months in storage.

HARVEST TIME Late Fall. Fruits may ripen over a seven- to ten-day period and require several pickings.

REGIONS WHERE GROWN The West Coast and the southeastern United States.

GROWING TIPS This very vigorous tree produces a dense canopy with somewhat upright branches. It does best on dwarfing rootstock in the home garden. Judicious pruning and training to open up the canopy benefit both the tree and its fruiting ability, especially fruit size and color. To achieve good fruit size, thin and space fruits adequately early in the season. This apple typically ripens after other late cultivars. In northern areas it may not mature before heavy frosts, and it will not ripen in regions with seasons shorter than 150 frost-free days after bloom. Fruits tolerate heat and do not sunburn readily. 'Cripps Pink' is winter hardy to minus 20°F. It is susceptible to apple scab and powdery mildew and very susceptible to fire blight. It should not be grown in regions where these diseases are prevalent unless stringent preventive measures are used.

—CR

'Devonshire Quarrendon'

This popular Victorian dessert apple is small to medium in size with thick, greasy, smooth skin that has a dark crimson-red flush and patches of green and yellow. Its flesh is white tinged with green or red and is very juicy, crisp, firm, sweet, and aromatic. Its flavor is reminiscent of strawberries, wine, or loganberries. First recorded in England in 1676, this apple is thought to be a native of Devon, England but may have originated in France. It is also called 'Red Quarrendon', 'Sack Apple', and some 35 other names.

CULINARY USES This excellent dessert apple also makes a good sauce and may be used for cider. As with most early apples, it does not keep well.

HARVEST TIME Pick it at its prime— early August to September; it's ripe when its seeds turn dark. If it's picked later, the fruit will be soft.

REGIONS WHERE GROWN This rare apple is grown in backyards by those who value its unusual flavor.

GROWING TIPS The tree is weakly growing and upright to spreading. Because of its low vigor and growth habit, it should not be grown on the most dwarfing rootstock. M.26 is a good choice. 'Devonshire Quarrendon' thrives in windy, rainy areas. It forms fruit on spurs and tends to bear a crop biennially, so thin every year to one fruit per spur and one fruit every six to eight inches. Prune out rapidly growing limbs (suckers) as soon as you see them. This early-flowering, self-sterile tree requires a pollinator such as 'Idared' and is a good pollinator for 'Gravenstein'. It is susceptible to scab. 'Devonshire Quarrendon' is hardy in Zones 5 to 7.

—TS

'Elstar'

The intense flavor of 'Elstar' and its very honeyed, sweet, crisp, juicy flesh descends from its grandparent 'Cox's Orange Pippin', one of the world's best apples. The medium to large, tender-skinned, round, yellow fruit is heavily covered with light red stripes. If it's picked in late August, it is tart; by early September it is sweeter; and by mid-September, it has developed a very good sweet-tart balance. Select the degree of tartness or sweetness you prefer by picking according to this schedule. 'Elstar' is a cross of 'Golden Delicious' and 'Ingrid Marie' (daughter of 'Cox's Orange Pippin') and was introduced in the United States in 1972. It is also called 'Lustre Elstar'.

CULINARY USES 'Elstar' is very good as a dessert apple and for cooking, and it makes great sauces and pies. Slices will fall apart in pies, but the apple holds its shape when baked or microwaved. Fruits can be stored for up to two

'Elstar' derives its intense flavor and honeyed, sweet flesh from its grandparent 'Cox's Orange Pippin'.

'Empire', a chance seedling of 'McIntosh', has become quite a popular variety in the Northeast. It resembles its parent in appearance and aromatic traits, but it holds up better in storage.

months when they are picked in September, keeping their flavor and crispness.

HARVEST TIME Late August to September.

REGIONS WHERE GROWN Pacific Northwest and the cooler regions of the United States, and portions of northeastern Canada.

GROWING TIPS The tree is moderately vigorous and the fruits are borne on spurs. Thin fruit and remove rapid-growing sprouts to overcome the variety's tendency to bear only biennially. 'Elstar' flowers late with an extended bloom period, making it a good pollinator for other mid- or late-flowering varieties such as 'Cox's Orange Pippin', 'Criterion', or 'Fiesta'. To control its size, try M.26 to M.9 rootstocks. 'Elstar' is moderately resistant to scab. it is hardy to Zone 5.

—*TS*

'Empire'

In 1941 a catastrophic spring frost eliminated most of New York's apple crop. Roger Way, an apple breeder at the Cornell University Agricultural Experiment Station, in Geneva, New York, collected some seeds from a small orchard of 'McIntosh' and 'Red Delicious' trees in the lower Hudson Valley that had escaped the freeze. 'Empire' was a serendipitous seedling from one of those trees, and it has since earned a place among the top newer varieties for the Northeast. It has the general appearance and aromatic traits of 'McIntosh', but it holds up better than its parent on the tree and in storage. 'Empire' fruits are dark red over pale green, medium sized, very crisp, mildly aromatic, and semitart.

CULINARY USES Best for fresh eating and cider; 'Empire' loses its texture in pies or sauces. It keeps well for three to five months.

Rather tart when first picked, spicy, sprightly 'Enterprise' mellows in storage. The apple was introduced in 1994 and is currently being evaluated throughout North America and Europe.

HARVEST TIME Early to mid-October.

REGIONS WHERE GROWN Mostly in New York, New England, Michigan, and Pennsylvania; occasionally in other apple-growing regions.

GROWING TIPS This moderately vigorous tree reliably sets most of its fruit on lateral spurs. It produces heavy crops but must be thinned aggressively to maintain adequate fruit size. It is moderately resistant to cedar-apple rust, powdery mildew, and fire blight but is susceptible to scab. 'Empire' is hardy in Zones 5 to 7.

—*IM*

'Enterprise'

These apples are very crisp, juicy, and flavorful, with a spicy, sprightly, tart taste—many people find them too tart. In storage, however, their tartness mellows. The fruits are large and round to slightly oblong, with a somewhat tough, chewy skin that is orange to red over a green or greenish-yellow undercolor. 'Enterprise', formerly known and tested widely as Coop-30, was released in 1994 as a controlled cross from the Purdue, Rutgers, and Illinois universities disease-resistant apple-breeding program (hence the letters *pri* in the apple's current name).

CULINARY USES This is a good dessert apple because of its crispness, juiciness, and full flavor; it is also good for cooking. Fruits can be stored for several months. If picked overripe or stored too long they develop a greasy surface.

HARVEST TIME Mid- to late autumn.

REGIONS WHERE GROWN This relatively new apple is being evaluated at many locations throughout North America and Europe.

GROWING TIPS 'Enterprise' grows vigorously and has a spreading habit, forming a round canopy crown. The tree does best on a precocious, size-controlling rootstock, on which it tends to bear at an earlier age. On large rootstock, it may take several years before the tree begins to bear a good crop regularly. Trees bloom in midseason, are not particularly prone to frosts, and require 170 to 190 days from bloom time for the crop to mature. This cultivar shows very strong resistance to multiple diseases; it is almost completely immune to apple scab and very resistant to cedar-apple rust, powdery mildew, and fire blight.

—CR

'Erwin Baur'

If you like sharp, tart apples, look no further. The especially hard flesh of 'Erwin Baur' is crisp, slightly aromatic, fine, and yellowish with a sweet to moderately acidic, aromatic flavor reminiscent of 'Cox's Orange Pippin'. The intensity of the acid flavor makes the mouth feel clean, like after eating a fine, smooth-tasting pickle. The medium-sized fruit is bright scarlet over a yellow background. This cross of 'Geheimrat Doktor Oldenburg' was raised in Brandenburg, in the former East Germany, and named in 1955.

CULINARY USES The intense flavor makes this an excellent dessert apple. In sauce it can easily compete with 'Gravenstein' and 'Bramley's Seedling'. The fruit keeps until the end of the year.

HARVEST TIME Late October.

Richly flavored and more tart than sweet, 'Esopus Spitzenburg' was reputedly one of Thomas Jefferson's favorite apples.

REGIONS WHERE GROWN Pacific Northwest and northern tier of the United States; southern Canada.

GROWING TIPS The tree is moderately vigorous and bears heavy crops. Grow it on a dwarfing rootstock (M.9 to M.26) to control its size. To prevent the tree from bearing biennially, thin the apples within 40 days of petal fall. 'Erwin Baur' blooms very early and is a good pollinator for 'Gravenstein' and 'Idared'; this trio would make an ideal pollination group for producing a great variety of tastes. It is resistant to apple scab.

—TS

'Esopus Spitzenburg'

This classic American dessert fruit originated in Esopus, in Ulster County, New York, in the late 18th century and was reputedly one of Thomas Jefferson's favorite apples. In 1790, he ordered a dozen trees from a Long Island nursery to plant at his Virginia home, Monticello, where he found it difficult to establish the trees due to the region's hot and humid growing conditions. At the Monticello Apple Tasting, which has been conducted each fall for more than

a decade, 'Esopus Spitzenburg' always ranks among the top five. The yellow flesh is rich, juicy, and more tart than sweet. The fruits are large, oblong, smooth skinned, and a lively, brilliant red approaching scarlet, specked with yellow. In hot and humid regions the color is less pronounced.

CULINARY USES This is a classic American variety for dessert; it is also used for pies, applesauce, baking, and drying.

HARVEST TIME Late September and early October.

REGIONS WHERE GROWN Pennsylvania northward to Maine and in the upper Midwest. In the warmer regions of the country the fruit flavor is diminished and the apple will keep only for a few weeks in storage; it is also subject to multiple diseases, particularly fire blight.

GROWING TIPS 'Esopus Spitzenburg' is moderately vigorous and upright with slender willowy limbs that have very desirable wide branch angles. This variety needs a pollinator like 'Golden Delicious', 'Grimes Golden', or a crabapple to increase fruiting. It bears a light crop of fruit every other year. Because of the variety's remarkable flavor, some orchardists struggle to grow 'Esopus Spitzenburg' in warmer regions anyway. This variety is susceptible to scab, mildew, and canker. If fruits are left on the tree too long, they can develop Jonathan Spot, brown, skin-deep marks that detract from its appearance but not its flavor. It is hardy in Zones 5 and 6 and the warmer parts of Zone 4.

—TB

Aromatic and spicy, 'Fameuse' is equally good for dessert, cooking, and cider. When grown from seed, it is one of the few varieties that produces offspring resembling its parent.

'Fameuse' or 'Snow Apple'

During the American Revolution a contingent of Hessian soldiers who were interned near Winchester, Virginia, planted an orchard with 'Fameuse' seeds, according to *Historic American Trees*. Sixteen of those trees were still bearing fruit in the 1930s. One of the remarkable merits of 'Fameuse' is that it is one out of thousands of apple varieties that reproduces its general likeness from seed. The apple was first noted in Canada in 1739 and is thought to have originated there in a seedling orchard from seeds brought from France, but even some French pomologists claim it originated in Canada. The coloration of 'Fameuse' varies, but generally it is solid red or pale yellow flushed red. The flesh is brilliant white, sometimes streaked red. It is aromatic with a spicy flavor. In the Mid-Atlantic states it is known solely as 'Snow Apple'. It is the probable parent of 'McIntosh' and is also known as 'Snow Chimney', 'Chimney Apple', 'Red American', 'Royal Snow', and 'Chimney Point'.

The homely looks of 'Freyberg' are deceiving. The creamy-white flesh of this variety has a firm texture and tastes very sweet with a spiciness that hints of anise.

CULINARY USES A versatile apple that's equally good for dessert, cooking, and cider. It is a long-keeping winter apple.

HARVEST TIME From late September to October.

REGIONS WHERE GROWN 'Fameuse' can be cultivated in all apple regions of the country.

GROWING TIPS The tree is medium in size but vigorous in growth, and the fruits are produced on short spurs. 'Jonathan' is a suitable pollinator to increase fruit production of 'Fameuse'. In the 19th century, the leaves were removed from around the best fruit on the tree to enhance their color. 'Fameuse' is susceptible to scab but less so than 'McIntosh'. It is hardy in Zones 4 to 7; in Zone 3, it is considered very hardy on Anatovka rootstock.

—TB

'Freyberg'

If you came upon this apple in a market, you wouldn't buy it—which is why you won't find it in markets. But once you've tasted this apple, you'll seek it out. The small to medium-sized fruit is unassuming, even ugly. Its skin is yellow-green with an occasional orange flush and some russeting around the stem cavity. But the juicy, aromatic, creamy-white flesh has a firm, fine texture and is very sweet, with a wonderful spicy flavor hinting of anise and a complex, lingering aftertaste. Its flavor intensifies as the apple ripens on the tree. 'Freyberg' is a New Zealand cross of 'Cox's Orange Pippin' and 'Golden Delicious' and was introduced in 1958. It is named after

Lord Freyberg, who was governor general of New Zealand from 1946 to 1952.

CULINARY USES 'Freyberg' is one of the better all-purpose apples for dessert, sauce, pies, baking, and salads. Use it soon after harvest.

HARVEST TIME Early October.

REGIONS WHERE GROWN 'Freyberg' tolerates summer heat and warm nights above the Mason-Dixon Line but also does well in cooler climates such as the Pacific Northwest.

GROWING TIPS Trees are medium sized and have weak vigor. A larger dwarfing rootstock like M.26 promotes adequate growth. The trees bear their fruit on spurs and will bear a light crop annually if thinned. They are self-sterile and require a pollinator such as 'Ginger Gold', 'Honey Crisp' or 'Melrose'. Fruit will hang well on the tree after it has ripened and can be harvested over several weeks. Restrict nitrogen, otherwise 'Freyberg' may not ripen properly. Apple stems are long, which makes it easy to bag the fruits for pest protection. The variety is susceptible to apple scab. It is hardy in Zones 5 to 7.

—TS

'Fuji'

This popular apple has a high sugar and low acid content, giving it a very mild, sweet flavor. The fine-textured, juicy flesh has a light cream color, and the skin ranges from mostly red striped to completely covered with a dark red blush, depending upon the strain of 'Fuji' grown. Fruits vary with environmental conditions from round to conical and are often a bit lopsided. Growers sometimes bag the fruits in paper bags to exclude light for much of the season. When they remove the bags a few weeks before harvest, the apples develop a bright pink-red color over a yellow undercolor. 'Fuji', a cross between 'Ralls Genet' and 'Golden Delicious', originated in Fujisaki, Japan, and was introduced in 1962.

CULINARY USES 'Fuji' is one of the most popular dessert apples because of its sweet flavor and good texture. When cooked, the fruits become somewhat bland. They store very well for several months in cold storage but will even last several weeks on a countertop; they soften with maturity.

HARVEST TIME Mid- to late autumn.

REGIONS WHERE GROWN The South and lower Midwest.

GROWING TIPS The 'Fuji' tree is vigorous and spreading. It tends to bear crops biennially, generally bearing fruit on terminal growths, but it is slow to start producing. It requires a long growing season for fruits to mature (approximately 160 to 180 days from bloom to harvest, almost two months after 'McIntosh') and is not suitable for regions with short growing seasons. 'Fuji' grows best in drier climates where disease pressure is low. The quality of the fruit is best in areas with warm days and cool nights during the ripening period. 'Fuji' may develop russet in humid areas, sunburn in intense, hot sunlight, and the stem or calyx cracks if rain is plentiful while the fruit is ripening. The variety is moderately susceptible to apple scab, susceptible to *Alternaria* leaf spot, and very susceptible to fire blight.

—*CR*

'Gala'

This apple is explosively crisp and juicy when ripe. The flavor of 'Gala' is excellent and well balanced: Some people consider it a sweet apple while others describe it as tart, but it really falls right

An excellent dessert apple considered sweet by some and tart by others, 'Gala' is best eaten fresh, as it becomes somewhat bland in cooking.

between the two. Fruits are small to medium sized, with somewhat glossy skin that has an attractive pink to red stripe over a yellow background. Newer 'Gala' strains are almost completely red to dark red. Fruits are round to slightly oval with yellow-cream color flesh and may have small, pronounced spots. 'Gala', a cross of 'Kidds Orange' and 'Golden Delicious', originated in New Zealand and was introduced in the United States in 1973.

CULINARY USES 'Gala' is among the best dessert apples, and though it's also good for cooking, the flavor may become somewhat bland. 'Gala' stores moderately well, maintaining texture and crispness, but flavor diminishes over time.

HARVEST TIME Late summer in the South to lower Midwest; early fall in the upper Midwest to northern regions. Fruits require several pickings over a 10- to 14-day period.

REGIONS WHERE GROWN All apple-growing regions.

GROWING TIPS 'Gala' is a vigorous tree with a somewhat spreading habit and need to be pruned annually to remove excess wood. The trees bloom early and prolifically over a period of several weeks. They may be susceptible to frost in frost-prone sites; their protracted bloom makes them good pollinators for other varieties. The tree tends to set a heavy fruit crop, so thin fruits to ensure good size. 'Gala' is among the most universally adapted apples, producing fruits of about the same size, color, and quality regardless of location. The variety is very susceptible to fire blight; it is susceptible to apple scab and powdery mildew.

—CR

'Golden Russet'

This antique apple of uncertain origin (probably a chance seedling from New York, circa 1840) was widely grown along the shores of Lake Ontario during the 1800s and was prized for its long keeping potential in the root cellar, its very high sugar content balanced by sprightly acidity, its strongly aromatic flavor, and its crisp, granular texture. 'Golden Russet' fell out of fashion in the early 1900s with the development of refrigerated storage and a growing preference for big, red apples. It is now much sought after at local farmers' markets for its rustic appearance and uniquely intense flavor.

CULINARY USES 'Golden Russet' can attain very high sugar levels but remains quite tart, resulting in a sugar-acid balance that is perfect for sweet or fermented ciders. It retains its texture and flavor in pies. It can be stored for three to five months.

HARVEST TIME Mid- to late October in the Northeast and somewhat earlier in

'Golden Russet' attains high sugar levels but remains quite tart, resulting in a sugar-acid balance that is perfect for sweet and fermented ciders.

Intense flavor, medium size, and a tendency to russet may keep 'GoldRush' out of supermarkets. But this scrumptious new apple is ideal for home growers, who will appreciate its disease resistance.

warmer areas of the Northwest and Mid-Atlantic. Pick the apples when the background color of the fruit changes from pale green to yellow.

REGIONS WHERE GROWN Throughout the Northeast; some plantings in the Northwest and Mid-Atlantic states. Wherever there are serious cider makers, this apple is grown.

GROWING TIPS 'Golden Russet' is a vigorous, sprawling tree that should be grown on dwarfing rootstock. Almost all the fruit is grown on the tips of the previous year's shoot growth, making the tree's branches droop like a willow tree. Minimal pruning of the previous year's shoots, combined with the removal of shaded older wood in the lower and inner canopy of the tree, promotes a good crop every year. Though somewhat resistant to scab, it is susceptible to cedar-apple rust and other common diseases. It does best in Zones 4 to 7.

—IM

'GoldRush'

'GoldRush' has a distinctively spicy flavor, a rare combination of intense acidity and high sugar content. In appearance, the medium-sized apple resembles its parent 'Golden Delicious'. The somewhat conical fruits are very firm in texture, yellow-green in background color, and lightly russeted, with a bright orange blush on their sunward cheek. The medium fruit size, intense flavor, and tendency to russet will probably keep this apple off the supermarket shelves, but it is ideal for home gardeners who want a disease-resistant apple with unique flavor that will keep for six months or more. 'GoldRush' is one of several dozen new apple varieties that are immune to apple scab (the result of four decades of cooperative fruit-breeding efforts at Purdue, Rutgers, and Illinois universities). Its scab immunity derives from a Siberian crabapple, and its complex pedigree includes 'Melrose' and 'Rome Beauty'.

CULINARY USES 'GoldRush' attains its full flavor after a month or two of refrigeration and is one of the longest-keeping apples. It is a multipurpose apple that makes excellent cider, is ideal for fresh salads or drying since it doesn't brown, maintains its flavor and firmness in pies, and is much appreciated for fresh eating by those who like a firm, very tart and sweet, intensely spicy apple.

HARVEST TIME End of October or early November.

REGIONS WHERE GROWN This new variety is not widely known but is catching on in the Mid-Atlantic region, in New York and New England, and in northern Italy.

GROWING TIPS 'GoldRush' trees are low in vigor. A semidwarf rootstock, such as M.7, is beneficial to maintain adequate tree vigor, and it will also help develop an ideal conical, open-limbed form with minimal pruning or branch positioning. 'GoldRush' comes into production quickly and bears annually, setting most of its fruit on spurs; aggressive thinning to one apple on every other spur is essential both for regular production and adequate fruit size. The tree is relatively resistant to fire blight and powdery mildew but susceptible to cedar-apple rust. It does best in Zones 5 to 7 and will not ripen properly in regions with short (fewer than 180 frost-free days) or long, hot growing seasons.

—IM

'Gravenstein'

This apple has yellowish-white flesh that is tender, fine-grained, and crisp, with a well-balanced acid-sugar content. Fruits are roundish and a bit lopsided with yellow skin marked with bright red and copper or orange. Soon after ripening, the skin develops a waxy or greasy feel. This apple is probably an Italian variety given to the Duke of Gravenstein in the 17th century; it arrived in Denmark in 1669. It was introduced in the United States from Germany in 1790. In 1820, 'Gravenstein' was planted at a Russian settlement in Sonoma County, California, and it has become so common in the United States, especially California, that it is sometimes considered an American variety. Among its many strains and cultivars are 'Mead', 'Red', 'Rosebrook', 'Washington', 'Australian', 'Yellow Striped', 'Blood Red', 'Shaw', and 'Crimson'.

CULINARY USES Suitable for pies and sauce making and as a highly flavored spicy and tart apple for fresh eating. Storage life is very short.

HARVEST TIME August to early September.

REGIONS WHERE GROWN New England and West Coast. Preharvest drop and diseases make it difficult to grow in the Mid-Atlantic states.

GROWING TIPS Grow this vigorous variety on a dwarfing rootstock like M.7 to keep the tree manageable. Prune and thin to control its tendency to bear a crop biennially. It blooms early and needs an early-blooming variety like 'Idared', 'Grimes Golden', or 'Liberty', to pollinate it. Pick it frequently because the apples ripen unevenly and tend to drop. Calcium deficiency can cause both bitter pit and water core. It is also subject to cedar-apple rust, scab, powdery mildew, and canker.

—TB

For a few blissful weeks in early fall, 'Gravenstein' makes its annual appearance. Be sure to enjoy these crunchy, juicy apples right away—they don't keep well at all.

'Grimes Golden'

Sometimes called 'Grimes Golden Pippin' or just 'Grimes', this variety was found in 1804 by Thomas Grimes in West Virginia, near a cider mill and nursery established by John Chapman—better known as Johnny Appleseed—and his brother. Trees of the variety can be found in abandoned orchards in Virginia, where after 50 years of neglect they are still bearing small, sooty-blotched fruit of extraordinary flavor. 'Grimes Golden' is believed to be one of the parents of 'Golden Delicious'. There are modern strains of 'Grimes Golden' that are larger in size but do not have the intense flavor of the original. (Inquire at the nursery about the source of the propagating material at the time of purchase.) The yellowish, coarse-grained flesh is crisp and tender with a spicy, sweet flavor. The fruits are roundish or slightly oblong and small to medium sized with a greenish-yellow skin ripening to a clear yellow, sometimes roughened with yellow or russet dots.

CULINARY USES A good all-purpose apple. its high sugar content made it

popular as the basis for hard cider and brandy in the Blue Ridge Mountains of Virginia. The fruits store well.

HARVEST TIME Mid- to late September.

REGIONS WHERE GROWN All apple-growing regions. The best-flavored, spiciest fruits are produced in the warmer zones of the Mid-Atlantic states.

GROWING TIPS 'Grimes Golden' is self-fertile and an excellent pollinator for other varieties. It tends to set an over-abundance of fruit and must be heavily thinned to produce large fruit. Heavy pruning to remove its bushy growth will also improve fruit production. In warmer regions the apples are larger and taste better. 'Grimes Golden' is subject to collar rot but is somewhat resistant to fire blight and cedar-apple rust. You can minimize collar rot with the dwarfing rootstock M9—which requires staking and irrigation—or by planting with the graft union at least two inches above ground level. It is hardy in Zones 6 to 8.
—*TB*

'Haralred'

This is a medium to small, round to conical apple with bright red skin sprinkled with round, whitish dots. The flesh is white, crisp, firm, juicy, and finely grained with a pleasant sweet-tart taste. 'Haralred' is a limb sport (a mutation of one cell that gives rise to a limb that is different from all other limbs on the parent tree) of the Minnesota variety 'Haralson'. It is also called 'La Crescent' and 'Minnesota'.

CULINARY USES 'Haralred' is very good for fresh eating. Its small core makes it

A good all-purpose apple high in sugar, 'Grimes Golden' was once popular as the basis for hard cider.

an excellent choice for sauces, pies, baking, and freezing. It will keep up to six months.

HARVEST TIME Late September in its southern range to mid-October in the Pacific Northwest.

REGIONS WHERE GROWN Northern United States and into Canada.

GROWING TIPS 'Haralred' does best in cold areas if it is grafted to a very hardy rootstock. Good choices in Zones 3 and 4 include P.22, P.2, O.3, and 'Anatovka'. A larger rootstock (M.26 or larger) counters the variety's natural dwarfing tendency. Trees often bear the first year after planting and will bear annually if thinned. If there's too much nitrogen in the soil, the fruits will not color or ripen properly. 'Haralred' is resistant to fire blight. This true northern apple can withstand extreme cold and is hardy in Zones 4 to 8 and into parts of Zone 3.
—TS

A relatively new variety, 'HoneyCrisp' has quickly gained many devotees, who enjoy its delicate flavor and juiciness.

'HoneyCrisp'

This new apple was developed by fruit breeders at the University of Minnesota and has quickly gained a devoted following around North America. It's currently the highest-priced apple in wholesale markets, fetching as much as a dollar per fruit. In favorable cool climates the fruit develops its uniquely appealing texture, delicate flavor, and juiciness, which remind some people of Asian pears. 'HoneyCrisp' was originally thought to be a cross between 'Macoun' and 'Honeygold', but recent genetic fingerprinting has shown that one of its parents was the variety 'Keepsake', and the other remains unknown.

CULINARY USES Excellent for eating fresh or using in fruit salads. Not well suited for cooking. When picked as they are just turning ripe, the fruits retain their quality in cold storage for up to six months.

HARVEST TIME Early to mid-September.

REGIONS WHERE GROWN 'HoneyCrisp' is being planted extensively in New England as well as in New York, Minnesota, Wisconsin, and the cooler upland valleys of central Washington.

GROWING TIPS 'HoneyCrisp' is not vigorous and does best on a semidwarf rootstock, such as M.7. It is prone to bear crops biennially, unless it is thinned in early summer to a single apple on every other spur. 'HoneyCrisp' leaves often develop yellow blotches during midsummer, but this leaf disorder does not appear to cause significant problems for the tree or fruit. This tree is susceptible to the common apple diseases and pests. Like other varieties from Minnesota, 'HoneyCrisp' is very tolerant of cold winters, and fruit quality is best when it is grown in cool regions, Zones 4 to 6.

—IM

'Hudson's Golden Gem'

This wild seedling was discovered near the Hudson Nursery in Tangent, Oregon, in 1931, and in texture and flavor it resembles the best antique russet apples of Europe such as 'St. Edmonds Pippin' or 'Egremont Russet'. The fruit is uniformly russeted, with crisp, white, granular flesh. It tastes mildly sweet and tart, with a nutty flavor resembling 'Bosc' pears. This variety has never achieved widespread commercial success, but it is often cited by apple lovers as one of their personal favorites.

CULINARY USES An excellent apple for fresh eating, salads, cooking, or cider. The fruit keeps for several months.

HARVEST TIME Mid-October.

REGIONS WHERE GROWN On both coasts of the United States in small plantings, and around the Great Lakes.

GROWING TIPS 'Hudson's Golden Gem' is a strong-growing tree that bears annually and is suitable for dwarf or semi-dwarf rootstocks. These grower-friendly traits along with high-quality russet fruit make it well worth a spot in the home garden. 'Hudson's Golden Gem' is quite resistant to scab and the other common apple diseases. It withstands winter cold and summer heat from Zones 3 to 8.

—IM

'Idared'

'Idared' apples are flattish to round, and their skin is a glossy, bright red over a green to greenish-white undercolor. The juicy, moderately crisp flesh is an attractive clear white with a fine texture and mild flavor that is tart to moderately acidic. Fruits are fragile and can bruise easily. 'Idared' was developed at the University of Idaho as a controlled cross of 'Jonathan' and 'Wagener' and introduced in 1942.

CULINARY USES This excellent cooking apple is used more often for baking and sauce than as a fresh apple. 'Idared' is also useful in cider blends. If they are harvested a few days early, the fruits can easily be stored for two to three months.

HARVEST TIME Mid- to late fall in the lower Midwest and upper South, at least four weeks after 'McIntosh'.

REGIONS WHERE GROWN Originally in the West but now popular in the Midwest and South.

Left: 'Hudson's Golden Gem' is mildly sweet and tart with a nutty flavor like 'Bosc' pears.

Right: Favored for baking and sauce, 'Idared' can be stored for several months.

GROWING TIPS This moderately vigorous tree has a spreading, almost weeping, growth habit and does well on dwarfing rootstock. It bears a good crop regularly and has been popular with many growers for that reason. It produces fruits in clusters on copious spurs and needs to be thinned to improve fruit size. Prune annually to encourage new growth and maintain vigor as well as fruit size, shape, and quality. 'Idared' requires about 160 to 170 days from bloom until harvest. It is moderately susceptible to apple scab and is susceptible to fire blight and powdery mildew. Mildew may cause a netted russet on the fruit. The fruits are also very susceptible to summer rots when they are ripe.

—CR

'Jonagold'

'Jonagold' has won many a taste test for its well-balanced flavor: Its high sugar and acid content perfectly complement each other. The fruits are aromatic, crisp, crunchy, and very juicy when ripe. The fruit color varies with season

and location from yellow-orange with pink highlights in warm to hot seasons or locations to luscious red over a yellow background in cooler years or climates. The fruits are round to slightly conical. In humid conditions they form some stem-end russet. 'Jonagold', introduced by the New York Agricultural Experiment Station, is a cross between 'Golden Delicious' and 'Jonathan'.

CULINARY USES 'Jonagold' is good for cooking, baking, and sauces, preserving both good texture and flavor. The fruits can be stored for a few months but lose flavor and texture over time and can become greasy.

HARVEST TIME Early fall. The fruits don't ripen uniformly and may require harvesting over a two-week period.

REGIONS WHERE GROWN Most fruit-growing regions, but especially coastal regions, the upper Midwest, Northeast, Northwest, and the mountainous regions of the South.

GROWING TIPS 'Jonagold' is a moderately vigorous tree, somewhat spreading, and produces large fruits, which are borne both on spurs and on short terminal shoots. Limbs respond well to positioning, making the tree a good choice for trellis or espalier forms. Prune annually to balance fruiting and wood growth. Thin the fruit every year to overcome the variety's tendency to bear biennially. A triploid variety, 'Jonagold' requires another cultivar that blooms at the same time to serve as a pollinator. It is also pollen sterile and cannot pollinate other cultivars. The tree requires 140 to 160 days from bloom to fruit maturation. Because 'Jonagold' sunburns readily, it

Well-balanced flavor and a crispy, crunchy texture make 'Jonagold' a popular dessert apple. But it's just as tasty cooked and in pies.

Firm, crisp, tender, juicy, and very aromatic, 'Jonathan' can be mild to tart. A treat to eat fresh and equally good cooked or baked, this variety is available for a short time in fall only.

does better in cooler climates; because of its vigor, it does best on dwarfing rootstocks when available. This variety is very susceptible to fire blight and susceptible to apple scab and powdery mildew. Fruits will form calcium deficiency–induced cork spot when grown too vigorously or in seasons with either very wet or dry spring conditions. Powdery mildew may cause fruit russet.

—*CR*

'Jonathan'

A medium to small, roundish apple with tough, thin, smooth skin, 'Jonathan' is bright yellow overlaid in bright to deep red, striped with carmine, with a fine russet netting. The whitish flesh is sometimes tinged red and is firm, crisp, tender, juicy, and very aromatic. The crisp cracking sound made by biting into 'Jonathan' along with the aroma and abundant juice, which fills the mouth, gives it its outstanding appeal. The apple's flavor varies from mild to tart and receives a very high ranking from apple aficionados. It is believed to be an 'Esopus Spitzenburg' seedling from the farm of Philip Rich, in Woodstock, New York, in the late 1700s. It quickly gained popularity because Jesse Buel, the president of the Albany Horticultural Society, favored it. He named it after Jonathan Hasbrouck, who had drawn his attention to the tree, which was growing in a scrubby spot on Rich's farm. It is also called 'King Philip', 'King Philipp', 'Philip Rich Ulster', and 'Ulster Seedling'.

CULINARY USES This apple is valued for pies and sauces as well as eating out of hand. 'Jonathan' retains its shape well when baked. The fruits keep poorly.

HARVEST TIME Mid-October.

REGIONS WHERE GROWN Highly adaptable to many climates from Michigan, Pennsylvania, Ohio, and Washington to southeastern Nebraska and the Pacific Northwest.

GROWING TIPS The tree is moderately vigorous, with a weeping, spreading habit, and bears its fruit on spurs. With proper thinning, it bears annually in rich, clay-loam soil. After five to eight years, some spurs need to be pruned to encourage more fruiting. Select the oldest spurs and head them back by a third to half. Be sure to prune no more than a quarter of the spurs each year. 'Jonathan' is resistant to apple scab and mildew but is susceptible to fire blight.
—TS

'Kandil Sinap'

This strikingly beautiful apple has porcelain-like, yellow-white skin with a brilliant reddish blush on the sunny side. The fruit is longish and cylindrical with tender, crisp, juicy, snow-white flesh. Its flavor is sweet and aromatic with plenty of fresh acidity. The tree grows like a Lombardy poplar, in a spire with a rounded base. 'Kandil Sinap' means "sweet apple of Sinope," and it is apparently named after the Sinop Peninsula, in Turkey, which juts into the Black Sea. This variety probably arose in the early 1800s and by around 1890 was a favorite in Turkey. It is also called 'Candil Sinap', 'Jubilee', 'Kandil', 'Kandile', 'Kantil Sinap', 'Sai Sinope', and 'Sinap Kandille'.

CULINARY USES This good to very good dessert apple is an excellent keeper that stores well through January.

HARVEST TIME Mid-October.

REGIONS WHERE GROWN Pacific Northwest and other regions as a novelty apple.

GROWING TIPS Grow this variety in the warmest of your microclimates. For good fruit production, train the branches of this upward-growing tree to 45- to 60-degree angles. The tree bears heavily every year, therefore thin the fruits so that they can develop their full flavor. 'Kandil Sinap' is self-sterile and requires a pollinator such as 'Liberty', 'Prima', or 'Prairie Spy'. On a larger rootstock (M.26 or larger) this tree will reach an adequate size. Its vigor is so low that it won't do well on dwarfing rootstock. It has little disease resistance. It is hardy in Zones 6 to 9.
—TS

A favorite in Turkey at the end of the 19th century, the cylindrical-shaped 'Kandil Sinap' is tender and crisp with snow-white flesh.

A cross of two tasty varieties, 'Cox's Orange Pippin' and 'Jonathan', 'Karmine' combines the best of both varieties, and it also keeps well, becoming sweeter over time.

'Karmine'

Nothing quite measures up to the complex, intense flavor and aroma of 'Karmine', a cross of 'Cox's Orange Pippin' with 'Jonathan', introduced from the Netherlands in 1971 as 'Karmine de Sonneville'. With its rich, nutty blend of acid and sugar, it is more intense even than its parent 'Cox's Orange Pippin'. The yellowish flesh is coarse, firm, juicy, and highly acidic. The fruit is medium to large, roundish, and variably shaped; the tough skin is partially red-orange over green-yellow, usually with russet around the flower end. The fruit may be ugly, but the flowers are large and beautiful.

CULINARY USES Great for baking and fresh eating and one of the best apples for juice. This apple keeps well and becomes sweeter over time.

REGIONS WHERE GROWN Pacific Northwest and in many places where 'Cox's Orange Pippin' can be grown.

HARVEST TIME Late September to mid-October.

GROWING TIPS The moderately vigorous tree has spreading thick branches and large leaves. Grow it on M.9 rootstock to control tree size. 'Karmine' bears annually if thinned. The tree produces sterile pollen (it is triploid) and thus requires a minimum of two other polli-

'Keepsake' may not be the prettiest apple, but it has a complex flavor, and, as its name suggests, it stores well for many months.

nators, one for 'Karmine' and one for the other pollinators. 'Melrose', 'Pristine', and 'Sweet Sixteen' are good choices. 'Karmine' has little disease resistance. It is hardy in Zones 5 to 9 and grows best in moist air where summers are not too hot or dry.

—TS

'Keepsake'

Like books, apples should not be judged by their covers, and 'Keepsake' will richly reward those who can appreciate the fine-grained, mildly acidic, very crisp, juicy flesh and rose petal–pineapple flavors that lie hidden beneath its humble exterior. The ripe fruits are medium to large and have sparse russeting and a dull red blush over a pale emerald background. A very cold-hardy apple variety developed at the University of Minnesota and introduced with little fanfare in 1979, this apple's name reflects both its long-term storage potential and its rustic, old-time appearance.

CULINARY USES Fruits are best for fresh eating but also good for pies, sauces, and cider. Like its more trendy offspring 'HoneyCrisp', this apple keeps for many months.

HARVEST TIME Mid-October.

REGIONS WHERE GROWN Not widely known outside Minnesota; very limited plantings in New England, New York, and Wisconsin.

GROWING TIPS Like its pollen parent 'Northern Spy', this is a strong-growing tree that takes several years to begin flowering and fruiting; then it will bear annually. Few commercial growers offer this variety, but its superb flavor and texture, its disease and cold resistance, and its long storage potential make it a natural choice for the home gardener who wants something uniquely satisfying, precious, and rarely available. Dwarfing rootstocks (M9, Bud9, or CG16) are ideal for 'Keepsake' in the home garden. The tree is resistant to fire blight and cedar-apple rust.

—IM

'King David'

This often overlooked antique apple should show up on lists of favorites for both growers and consumers. Its aromatic fruits have yellow to light cream flesh that is very firm to hard; it is crisp and juicy with an old-fashioned spicy, ciderlike flavor. The occasional argument over whether this is a sweet or tart apple indicates some seasonal variation and a well-balanced combination of sugars and acids. Fruits are medium to large, round, and very dark red with darker red stripes over a pale green undercolor. The skin is somewhat tough and the flesh has a coarse texture that is hard to almost woody. It softens as it ripens as well as in storage. The tree originated as a chance seedling in Arkansas in the late 19th century and is thought to be a cross of 'Jonathan' and either 'Winesap' or 'Arkansas Black'.

CULINARY USES Good for dessert, cooking, or cider. 'King David' holds up well in baking and makes a flavorful, coarse sauce and flavorful cider alone or when blended. Fruits store well for months. When overripe or stored too long, they become very waxy to greasy.

HARVEST TIME Mid- to late autumn; fruits hang on the tree well and can be harvested for several weeks.

An antique variety with a ciderlike flavor, 'King David' is a versatile apple that is hard when first harvested and softens over time.

REGIONS WHERE GROWN An antique cultivar of the South that is also grown in New England, the Mid-Atlantic, Midwest, West Coast, and elsewhere.

GROWING TIPS The tree is moderately vigorous, somewhat spreading, and more tolerant of abuse, environmental problems, and neglect than many other varieties. 'King David' blooms late, which makes it a good choice for apple growers in regions with spring frosts. It benefits from cross-pollination and is a good pollinator for other late-blooming cultivars such as 'Arkansas Black' and 'Rome Beauty'. 'King David' is widely adapted; it grows well in the heat and sun of the South and tolerates humid conditions, but it needs extended warm autumn weather for the fruits to mature. It does well on dwarfing rootstocks when available. Since the fruits turn a rich, dark red color before they are fully ripe, it's easy to pick them too early, before their flavor is at its best. 'King David' has very low susceptibility to fire blight and is almost completely resistant to apple scab and cedar-apple rust. It does not sunburn in summer heat and sun.

—CR

The 'Lady Apple' is a tiny variety, but so much fresh flavor is packed in its shiny skin that its popularity has endured for centuries.

'Lady Apple'

One of the first European apples brought to America, 'Lady Apple' is thought to have been found in the Forest of Api, in Brittany, France. It was first recorded in 1628, though some enthusiasts think it could be the Appian apple of the Roman Empire, described by Pliny the Elder in the first century AD. In North America, the variety flourished, and after the Civil War, barrels of 'Lady Apple' were exported from Virginia to England, where they commanded the phenomenal price of up to $30 per barrel, four times more than other varieties. The flesh of 'Lady Apple' is tender, white, crisp, and very juicy, with much of the flavor in the skin. The fruit is small and flattish with a shiny skin that ranges from creamy or ivory yellow in the shade to a deep glossy crimson on the sun-exposed side. In France, it's been called 'Nome Api' for three centuries. In Quebec, it's known as 'Petit Api', 'Pomme d' Api', and 'Pomme Rose'. It is also called 'Lady's Finger', 'Christmas Apple', 'Lady Sweet', and dozens of other names. The larger cultivars—'Black Lady Apple', 'Star Lady Apple', 'Large Lady Apple', 'Rose-Colored Lady Apple', and the seedlings 'Helen' and 'Highland Beauty'—are considered to be of lesser quality.

CULINARY USES For dessert, cooking, cider making, and decoration, especially for wreaths and garlands during the winter holiday season. 'Lady Apple' stores well for two or three months.

HARVEST TIME Late October and early November. This is usually one of the last varieties picked. The fruits survive repeated freezing and thawing on the tree.

REGIONS WHERE GROWN All apple-growing regions of the country.

GROWING TIPS The 'Lady Apple' tree is upright in growth and bears its fruit in clusters. Use limb spreaders to expose the fruit to sunlight and improve color and permit air circulation to reduce disease. Cross-pollination with cultivars like 'Golden Delicious', 'Grimes Golden', 'Winter Banana', and many crabapples improves fruit production. This cultivar is slow to begin bearing, but once production begins, fruiting is heavy. It tends to fruit biennially: A tree may have six bushels one year and only six apples the next. 'Lady Apple' is susceptible to scab. It is hardy in Zones 5 to 7.

—TB

'Liberty'

'Liberty' develops a deep purple color overlaid with silver bloom (a natural waxy layer). It is a tart apple with a winelike aroma and mild astringency that adds a pleasant finish to sweet and fermented ciders. This modern apple was developed at Cornell University's fruit-breeding program in Geneva, New York. It is a cross between 'Macoun' and Purdue 54-12 and was introduced in 1978.

CULINARY USES This all-purpose apple is suitable for fresh eating, pies, sauces, and processing. 'Liberty' maintains fresh-eating quality for only a few months in refrigerated storage; it tastes best when fully ripened on the tree.

HARVEST TIME Early October.

Tart and mildly astringent with a winelike aroma, 'Liberty' is a good all-purpose apple that adds a nice finishing touch to cider.

REGIONS WHERE GROWN Mainly New York and New England.

GROWING TIPS 'Liberty' is a vigorous upright tree that should be grown on dwarfing rootstocks in full sun. The tree also requires judicious pruning and branch positioning during its formative years. It is very productive and bears a good crop annually, but it must be thinned to one apple per spur to maintain good fruit size and prevent losses to preharvest fruit drop. This tree is a mainstay variety that will come through when others fail in the home garden. Its high level of resistance to the major apple diseases is unsurpassed by any other variety. Unfortunately, insect pests seem to find its fruit especially attractive. It is immune to scab. 'Liberty' is well suited to Zones 5 to 7.

—IM

Not well known outside the Northeast, where it is much sought after, 'Macoun' melts gently on the tongue, releasing a mildly spiced juice and floral acidity quite unlike any other apple.

'Macoun'

Expatriate New Englanders reminisce longingly about 'Macoun', which does not ship well to distant markets or retain its delightful flavor long enough to store long term. Its distinctive snowy flesh melts gently on the tongue, releasing a mildly spiced juice and floral acidity quite unlike any other apple. 'Macoun' (pronounced like *McGowen*) is not well known outside the Northeast. One of the first apples developed by Cornell's Geneva Experiment Station, it is a cross between 'McIntosh' and 'Jersey Black' and was released in 1923.

CULINARY USES 'Macoun' is best for fresh eating, but it also makes good sauce, pie filling, and cider.

HARVEST TIME Early October.

REGIONS WHERE GROWN Almost exclusively in New York and the New England states, although 'Macoun' can certainly be grown in other regions in Zones 4 to 7.

GROWING TIPS 'Macoun' is a strong-growing, erect tree that produces abundant spurs but few secondary lateral branches. It is best grown on a dwarfing rootstock. Its wood is stiff and does not bend easily, so early pruning and branch spreading are essential to develop a form that allows air and sunlight to penetrate throughout the tree and thus minimize the fungal problems to which 'Macoun' is susceptible. The tree may suffer substantial preharvest drop if it is not thinned to one fruit per spur during early summer or when it is buffeted by winds and warm weather during maturation. Fruit quality is best in cooler growing regions where days are sunny and nights are cool during autumn.

—IM

'Mammoth Blacktwig'

'Mammoth Blacktwig' is an antique apple with crisp, firm flesh that's juicy and somewhat tart. Fruits are large and round with bright to dark red over a yellow background and pronounced yellow to white spots. They may have russet in the calyx and stem end. 'Mammoth Blacktwig' is thought to have originated as a 'Winesap' seedling in Washington County, Arkansas, on the farm of John Crawford in 1842. It resembles 'Winesap' in both the tree and the fruit. 'Mammoth Blacktwig' may also be called 'Blacktwig', 'Big Blacktwig', 'Arkansaw', and 'Big Winesap'.

CULINARY USES 'Mammoth Blacktwig' can be used as a fresh dessert apple, but it also cooks very well. Its tartness makes it good for drying or for cider blends. Fruits get sweeter as they mature and can be stored for a long period, but they will become mealy after more than three to four months.

HARVEST TIME Mid- to late fall.

REGIONS WHERE GROWN The South and Midwest.

GROWING TIPS The tree is moderately vigorous with a round, spreading canopy. It produces thick wood and large leaves, often with a dense canopy. The tree blooms in mid- to late season and may escape frosts as a result; it requires about 160 to 190 days from bloom until harvest. 'Mammoth Blacktwig' is resistant to fire blight, cedar-apple rust, and many fruit harvest rots but susceptible to apple scab and superficial sooty blotch and flyspeck. The foliage and fruit are somewhat resistant to insect pests.

—CR

Its tartness makes 'Mammoth Blacktwig' a good candidate for drying or cider blends. It's equally delightful for fresh eating.

'McIntosh'

'McIntosh' was widely planted after the devastating freeze of the winter of 1934–35 that destroyed many 'Baldwin' orchards. This apple has white flesh, sometimes tinged red. It is fine, crisp, and tender with a moderately acidic to sweet and spicy taste that has become known as the classic 'McIntosh' flavor. The medium to large fruit has pale yellow skin flushed and striped a deep, bright red and covered with a bloom— a grayish dust over the surface of the apple. The skin and flesh have a perfumed scent. 'McIntosh' was discovered in 1796 by John McIntosh near Dundela, in Dundas County, Ontario, Canada. It was then propagated by Allan McIntosh and introduced in 1870. Before 1835 it was called 'Gem'.

CULINARY USES 'McIntosh' is the all-purpose apple of New England. It is excellent fresh as well as for cooking and cider making.

HARVEST TIME Mid- to late September.

REGIONS WHERE GROWN It is restricted to the cooler zones but grows particularly well in New England.

GROWING TIPS The vigorous tree sets heavy crops, is self-fertile, and blooms early. It is also a good pollinator for other varieties. In the Mid-Atlantic states it grows well at elevations over 1,000 feet. At lower elevations the apples become mealy soon after ripening. 'McIntosh' sometimes ripens unevenly and is subject to preharvest drop. It has been grown on dwarfing rootstock with mixed results. It is susceptible to scab. 'McIntosh' is hardy in Zones 4 to 6 and if protected, in some parts of Zone 3.

—*TB*

Rather tart when it is first picked in fall, 'Melrose' transforms into a sweet dessert apple by the end of the year and can be stored for up to six months.

'Melrose'

'Melrose' is large, flattish, and shiny red over yellow-green, with white, crisp flesh that is somewhat acidic and sweet. 'Melrose', introduced in 1944, is a cross of 'Jonathan' and 'Red Delicious' by Freeman S. Howlett, at the Ohio Experiment Station, in Wooster, Ohio. It is the official apple of Ohio.

CULINARY USES This excellent sweet dessert apple is best eaten at the end of the year, but they are delicious tart, right off the tree. The cooked flesh is tender and velvety and retains its shape and flavor when baked in a pie. It is also good in salads and for cider. Fruits keep for up to six months.

HARVEST TIME Mid-October to November.

REGIONS WHERE GROWN Pacific Northwest but highly adaptive to other areas.

GROWING TIPS 'Melrose' is a good choice for damp, humid climates. The vigorous tree has an upright-spreading growth pattern and bears fruits while young. Grow it on M.9 to M.26 rootstocks to control size. Restrict nitrogen use after the first three to four years, otherwise fruits will not develop or color well. Fruits require sunlight for color, so create extra space between branches when pruning. Thin to one fruit per cluster to produce an annual crop (the stem is so short that multiple fruits will crowd each other out). This

In fall, the perfumed scent of freshly harvested 'McIntosh' apples wafts through many orchards in New England, where it is one of the most popular varieties grown.

late-flowering tree does best with a pollinator such as 'Mother', 'Redfree', or 'Spartan'. It is very resistant to fire blight and slightly susceptible to powdery mildew and anthracnose. It is hardy in Zones 5 to 9 but not suitable for areas that experience excessive heat.

—TS

'Mutsu'

This apple's fine granular texture, subtle anise aroma, and mildly astringent semi-tart flavor have gained it an appreciative following in the Northeast. The fruits are pale green, changing to yellow with a light orange blush on the sunny side as they ripen. They rarely develop russet. They can be very large (a trait valued highly in Japan), especially on young or heavily thinned trees. 'Mutsu', a cross between 'Golden Delicious' and 'Indo', was an early release (1948) from the fruit-breeding program at the Aomori Experiment Station in northern Japan. It is also known as 'Crispin'.

CULINARY USES This is an excellent apple for fresh eating. It remains firm in pies and makes a fine sweet or hard cider. This excellent keeper's fine qualities are retained for up to five months in storage.

HARVEST TIME Mid-October.

REGIONS WHERE GROWN Mostly in Japan, New York, Michigan, California, and the New England states, as well as in a few orchards in England and France.

GROWING TIPS 'Mutsu' is a vigorous and spreading tree in its early years, but it settles down quickly when it begins fruiting. It performs very well on dwarfing rootstocks. Growers often choose not to thin 'Mutsu', accepting the tree's slight tendency to bear crops biennially in order to keep fruit size smaller and more manageable. Mature trees require relatively little dormant pruning and can tolerate rather infertile soils. This is a triploid variety (a trait linked with large leaves and fruit) and will not pollinate other varieties. 'Mutsu' is an excellent choice for the home garden and will reward the grower with many years of impressive fruit for the table. It is resistant to powdery mildew but susceptible to other diseases, including a bacterial blister spot on its fruit in some locations. It is well adapted in Zones 5 to 7.

—IM

'Newtown Pippin'

'Newtown Pippin' is one of the world's classic apple varieties. Its yellowish flesh is very firm, crisp, juicy, and moderately acidic with a clean, fresh taste. Two distinct strains, a green and a yellow one, were differentiated as early as 1817. 'Albemarle' and those with "yellow" in the name, such as

A subtle anise aroma and mildly astringent semitart flavor are the hallmarks of 'Mutsu', also known as 'Crispin', a rather large cultivar developed in Japan.

Moderately acidic with a clean, fresh taste, 'Newtown Pippin' is a classic winter apple that comes into its own after a few months of storage.

'Yellow Newtown' and 'Yellow Pippin', are generally designated the yellow type; 'Brooke' and those with green in the name, such as 'Green Winter' or 'Green Newtown', are the green type. However, positive identification is often difficult, as soil conditions and weather can determine appearance and taste. The fruit varies in color and size but is usually medium to large and solid green becoming a yellow or greenish yellow with a reddish blush. It may be russeted around the basin with small russet dots over the surface of the fruit, which is roundish, flattened, and angular with a short stem. It is thought to have originated early in the 18th century in New York on the Newtown, Long Island, estate of Gershom Moore, whose ancestors may have brought it as

a seed or young tree from England about 1666. The original tree died in 1805 from excessive cutting of propagation wood. By the mid-19th century, barrels of 'Newtown Pippin' grown on the eastern slopes of the Blue Ridge Mountains in Virginia were being shipped to England and commanding a price higher than that of any other apple. During the reign of Queen Victoria, 'Newtown Pippin' was the only food commodity exempt from the crown import tax, reportedly because the court so liked the flavor. George Washington and Thomas Jefferson both extolled the virtues of the variety.

CULINARY USES 'Newtown Pippin' is an all-purpose apple that develops optimum flavor after a few months of storage. The flesh oxidizes quickly after cutting, so it is not suitable for salads. During export to England in the 19th century, the long sea voyage likely enhanced the flavor. Cider made from the fruit is very clear and considered of the highest quality. With proper storage, the apples will last until April. Begin eating them in January or February when the flavor is at its zenith.

HARVEST TIME October.

REGIONS WHERE GROWN In New England as 'Newtown Pippin', in Virginia as 'Albemarle Pippin', and on the West Coast as 'Yellow Newtown Pippin'.

GROWING TIPS The shoots on the vigorous tree grow to medium length and fairly straight but upright. Use limb spreaders to open up the tree canopy. It is susceptible to scab infection and powdery mildew but shows resistance to collar rot. It is hardy in Zones 5 to 8.

—TB

'Northern Spy'

One of the best varieties for storing, these apples are large, especially on young trees, with white, very juicy, crisp, tender, and sweet flesh with a rich, aromatic, mildly acidic flavor. The fruit is a clear yellow with bright red tints, although there can be regional variability in the appearance. 'Northern Spy' was found in an orchard at East Bloomfield, New York, grown from seedlings brought from Connecticut about 1800. It may originally have been called 'Northern Pie Apple' and is also known as 'Red Spy' and 'Red Northern Spy'. It has been selected for use in the development of new varieties and in rootstock research.

CULINARY USES 'Northern Spy' is good for fresh eating, pies, sauce, and cider.

HARVEST TIME Late September and early October.

REGIONS WHERE GROWN From Maine southward to the mountains of Virginia and North Carolina, as well as the upper Midwest and the West Coast.

GROWING TIPS This very hardy tree has an upright, brushy growth habit with long curved branches and dense foliage. Use limb spreaders to open the canopy to sunlight and air circulation. It is notorious for being slow to begin bearing. On standard rootstock, ten years may expire before the first harvest, but on a dwarfing rootstock the tree usually begins to bear in three to four years. During rainy weather the fruit may crack, and during harvest it is easily bruised because of its delicate skin. 'Northern Spy' blooms late and escapes frost. Late-blooming pollinators like 'York', 'Wealthy', and 'Ralls Genet' will increase fruiting. Some orchardists claim that trees planted in grass sod begin to

'Northern Spy' is a very juicy, large apple that easily keeps for several months.

bear earlier than those planted where the soil under the tree has been cultivated at the time of planting. Too much nitrogen in the soil will diminish the flavor of the apple. 'Northern Spy' is subject to apple scab, bitter pit, and fire blight. It is hardy in Zones 4 to 6.

—TB

'Ozark Gold'

'Ozark Gold' has become popular at farmers' markets, roadside stands, and in home gardens. The fruits are round and bright yellow when ripe. The skin has a very smooth, glossy finish and in cooler conditions may form a kiss of pink blush on the cheek. 'Ozark Gold' is moderately crisp and juicy with a mild flavor. Completely ripe fruits are a bit soft, very waxy, not quite greasy, and polish very attractively. If the fruits are harvested "firm," they are often greenish in color and will not have developed their full flavor. Fruits do color well in the summer heat, but they will drop off the tree just as they ripen if temperatures are too warm. 'Ozark Gold' was developed by the Missouri State Experiment Station as a cross between 'Golden Delicious' and the seedling of a 'Conrad' and 'Delicious' cross. Released in 1970, it never achieved the notoriety of its parent or developed a large commercial following. Nonetheless, it is a cultivar worth growing.

CULINARY USES This apple is best for fresh eating. Even though it is attractive when cooked, its flavor is weak and it makes a bland sauce or pie filling. Fruits don't store well for more than a month or so, losing flavor and texture with time.

HARVEST TIME 'Ozark Gold' is considered a late-summer apple; it ripens at about the same time as 'Gala' and two to three weeks before 'Golden Delicious'. It requires about 110 to 120 frost-free days from bloom until harvest. The fruits ripen over a ten-day period.

A late-summer apple, 'Ozark Gold' is best enjoyed for about a month after harvest.

REGIONS WHERE GROWN A native of the Ozarks, this apple is grown throughout the lower Midwest and in the foothills of the Appalachians in the Southeast.

GROWING TIPS The moderately vigorous tree with wide branch angles has a tendency to set too much fruit and produce small apples. For a more moderate crop of larger apples, thin the fruits soon after bloom. This also allows the flower buds for the following year's crop to develop. 'Ozark Gold' has a relatively long bloom period and is often a complementary pollinator apple for other cultivars. It has little disease resistance and is susceptible to scab, cedar-apple rust, powdery mildew, and fire blight.

—CR

With its notes of licorice and pineapple, 'Priscilla' adds a distinctive flavor to cider blends. But the apple's unusual flavor is not for everyone.

'Priscilla'

'Priscilla' has crisp, granular flesh, is semitart and has an unusual licorice and pineapple aroma and flavor that people tend to either love or hate. This cross between 'Starking Delicious' and PRI610-2 was an early release from the Purdue/Rutgers/Illinois universities cooperative fruit-breeding program, introduced in 1972. An unfortunate mix-up with an inferior variety during the initial distribution led many growers to reject this apple; for home gardeners it definitely deserves consideration. 'Priscilla' is a medium-sized, conical apple, with carmine stripes over a creamy-white background when ripe.

CULINARY USES 'Priscilla' is suitable for all uses; it remains firm when baked and adds a distinctive flavor to cider blends. Fruits can be stored for two to three months in refrigeration without loss of flavor or firmness.

HARVEST TIME Late September. The fruits ripen over a two- to three-week period and hang well on the tree, with few apples dropping prematurely.

REGIONS WHERE GROWN Not widely known, this apple is grown mostly in the Midwest and Mid-Atlantic states and in a few New York and New England orchards.

GROWING TIPS 'Priscilla' is an easy tree to grow. Moderately vigorous, it begins fruiting quickly and produces annual crops consistently. It develops an open spindle tree form with minimal training in the early years. Thin the fruit to one per spur to improve their size and flavor. Prune out older shaded spur clusters on mature trees to maintain shoot growth and encourage renewal. 'Priscilla' will reward home gardeners who appreciate its unique flavor with abundant crops and few troubles. It is immune to scab and resistant to other apple diseases. This variety is among the most disease-resistant introductions of the Purdue/Rutgers/Illinois program and is reliably hardy in Zones 5 to 8.

—IM

'Ralls Genet'

The yellowish flesh of 'Ralls Genet' is dense, crisp, and tender with a flavor that balances tart and sweet. When cut, the flesh exudes a sweet aroma. The fruit is medium sized and roundish. Its greenish-yellow skin is flushed, mottled, and streaked various shades of pink, red, and crimson, with yellow and white dots speckling its surface. Scarfskin, a patchy thin scar-tissue layer over the skin, may appear on some fruit. Inside the basin around the stem, the fruit is usually russeted. 'Ralls Genet' reportedly was found growing on the farm of Caleb Ralls in Amherst County, Virginia, in the late 1700s. It was one of the American varieties imported by the Japanese to establish an apple-breeding program. (It is called 'Kokko' in Japan). From a cross of 'Ralls Genet' and 'Red Delicious' came 'Fuji', now a major commercial variety. 'Ralls Genet' is also widely grown in China, particularly in the northern provinces. It is frequently called 'Ralls Janet', simply 'Ralls', and 'Neverfail'.

CULINARY USES 'Ralls Genet' is an all-purpose apple, but it is especially suitable for fresh eating and for cider. It stores throughout the winter months.

HARVEST TIME Early October.

REGIONS WHERE GROWN Throughout the apple-producing areas of the country.

GROWING TIPS Because it blooms so late in the season, this is the apple variety of choice for areas with late frosts. 'Ralls Genet' grows well in both clay and loam soils. On seedling rootstock the tree always remains small, but even on hybrid rootstock it is not a vigorous grower. The tree has a rather brushy habit and requires pruning to open up the canopy to air circulation and sun-light. It sets a heavy crop annually, so thin severely to increase fruit size. It is susceptible to scab, blossom blight, and bitter rot. The tree seems to be very resistant to collar rot. 'Ralls Genet' is hardy in Zones 5 to 8.

—TB

'Rhode Island Greening'

'Rhode Island Greening' is the American apple that should replace 'Granny Smith' in pie recipes. Its greenish-yellow flesh is finely textured and firm with an acid flavor. The fruit is medium to large and ribbed at the blossom end and on the body; the green skin may have a brownish or orange blush with russet at the base and pale russet dots. This "very large fair apple," has a flesh "yellowish, firm, moderately fine-grained, crisp, tender, juicy, rich, sprightly subacid," wrote S.A. Beach in his 1905 *Apples of New York*. It was known by 1650 and probably originated at Green's End, in Newport, Rhode Island. It is also called 'Burlington Greening', 'Russine', 'Ganges', 'Greening', 'Green Newtown Pippin', 'Green Winter Pippin', and 'Jersey Greening'.

The perfect pie apple, 'Rhode Island Greening' turns a golden brown when cooked and has a fine and tender texture.

grown in combination with two different pollen-producing trees, such as 'Golden Delicious' and McIntosh'. Harvest the apples before the skin begins to turn yellow. In some soils and climates, preharvest drop may occur. In warmer areas, the tree produces better-quality fruit at elevations over 1,000 feet. Scab and some cankers are problems, and some damage from blossom and twig blight may occur. 'Rhode Island Greening is hardy in Zones 5 to 7.

—*TB*

CULINARY USES When cooked in a pie filling or otherwise, the fruit becomes a golden brown and the texture is fine and tender. After a few months of storage, the sprightly, tart taste develops and it is suitable for fresh eating. 'Rhode Island Greening' stores through the winter months.

HARVEST TIME September and early October.

REGIONS WHERE GROWN Premium crops of 'Rhode Island Greening' are produced in New England, but good- to fair-quality fruit is also grown in the Mid-Atlantic states.

GROWING TIPS Vigorous and long lived—on standard rootstock a 'Rhode Island Greening' can live to be 150 years old—the tree is slow to begin bearing and has a tendency to bear biennially. This poor pollen producer should be

'Rome Beauty'

This very old apple is still a favorite with both growers and consumers. The large fruits are round and bright to dark red over a green to white undercolor. The white flesh is firm to hard and very crisp and juicy with a sprightly, aromatic flavor. The apple was first described and named in 1846 in Rome Township, Ohio, near the Ohio River.

CULINARY USES This apple can be eaten fresh as a dessert apple, but the tough, thick skin and firm to woody texture of the flesh can be unappealing. 'Rome Beauty' is excellent for baking or frying, and it's a good cider-blend apple. Fruits can easily be stored for two to three months, but after four months in storage they become soft and mealy, though they may still retain a good apple flavor.

HARVEST TIME Mid- to late autumn.

REGIONS WHERE GROWN Originally the Midwest; now in almost all apple-growing regions.

Ever popular 'Rome Beauty' is an old variety well suited to cooking and ciders. It is often less appealing for fresh eating—its skin can be hard and thick and the flesh rather woody.

GROWING TIPS 'Rome Beauty' is a mid-sized tree with a weeping growth habit that begins producing fruits early and bears reliably. It responds readily to training and trellising. Prune the tree by removing nonproductive, vigorous growth. Don't head back branches, since the tree bears fruits from buds on shoot terminals. To induce greater flower formation, reposition limbs from a vertical to a more horizontal angle. Because of its late bloom time, this variety needs a late-blooming complementary cultivar for cross pollination, such as 'Arkansas Black' and 'King David'. It is very susceptible to cedar-apple rust, powdery mildew, and fire blight. After infection with fire blight, the wood may develop other wood rots. Cedar-apple rust may be so severe in some regions and seasons as to almost defoliate trees by midsummer. 'Rome Beauty' is also susceptible to apple scab. Because of its late maturity, it cannot be grown in regions with short seasons and early fall frosts.

—CR

'Roxbury Russet'

Thought to be the oldest named apple variety from America, 'Roxbury Russet' is a classical apple of the French "reinette" type, featuring conspicuous spots. It originated as a chance seedling in Massachusetts in the early 1600s. The fruits are large and round, with light brown russeting over a green background that changes to pale yellow as the apples ripen. Its white flesh is crunchy and granular; its flavor is sweet and also very tart. Like 'Golden Russet', this was once a very popular apple in the Northeast that fell out of favor but is again in demand at farmers' markets and specialty-produce retailers.

CULINARY USES 'Roxbury Russet' is excellent for fresh eating, pies and sauces, and as a cider blend. It holds up well for three to five months.

REGIONS WHERE GROWN Mostly in New England and New York, in limited small plantings by fans of antique apples.

HARVEST TIME Mid-October.

GROWING TIPS 'Roxbury Russet' is a vigorous tree that does best on dwarfing rootstock. It produces abundant new shoots annually when grown in good soil and needs judicious pruning every year. It bears a good crop of fruit on both spurs and shoot tips. Preharvest drop can be a problem. It is somewhat resistant to scab, mildew, and fire blight. It is suitable for Zones 5 to 7.

—IM

'Sansa'

One of the finest-flavored early-maturing apples, 'Sansa' originated

Crunchy, granular, sweet and also very tart, 'Roxbury Russet' used to be much in demand, fell out of favor, and is now making a comeback.

A sweet and flavorful apple that ripens early and also stores well, 'Sansa' is becoming a popular choice at farmers' markets and pick-your-own orchards.

from a cooperative breeding program involving apple breeders in New Zealand and the Morioka Station in Japan. A cross between 'Gala' and 'Akane', it was introduced in 1986. This apple is superior to most other early-ripening varieties in flavor and storage potential. It resembles its parent 'Gala' somewhat in appearance and size. Its skin is lightly russeted and blushed with orange, and it has crisp, granular flesh, lots of sugar and flavor, and little acidity. 'Sansa' is relatively unknown commercially but is becoming popular at farmers' markets and pick-your-own orchards.

CULINARY USES Suitable for fresh eating, pies, and cider, this is truly an all-purpose apple.

HARVEST TIME Late August in the Northeast and somewhat earlier in warmer regions such as central Washington and California.

REGIONS WHERE GROWN Mostly in Japan, New York, California, and elsewhere in small plantings.

GROWING TIPS Erect in form and not very vigorous, 'Sansa' has rather brittle branches that should be trained horizontally during the early years to avoid breakage under subsequent crop loads. It comes into production quickly and is well suited to either dwarf or semidwarf rootstocks. The leaves of 'Sansa' often develop yellow flecking, which is harmless to the tree and the fruit. 'Sansa' is an easy apple to grow and will get your apple season off to a great start. It is immune to scab and resistant to powdery mildew and fire blight. It is suited to Zones 5 to 8.

—IM

'Smokehouse'

This large blocky apple has a red-flushed, greenish-yellow skin with carmine stripes and plenty of russet dots on the surface. The yellowish-white flesh is dense, chewy, and tender with a mildly acidic flavor. The variety supposedly originated near a smokehouse on the farm of William Gibbons, near Millcreek, Pennsylvania, in the early 1800s and is thought to be a seedling of 'Vandevere'. 'Smokehouse' is also called 'English Vandevere', 'Gibbons Smokehouse', 'Millcreek Vandevere', 'Millcreek', and 'Red Vandevere'.

CULINARY USES When picked in late August, 'Smokehouse' is mature enough for cooking; by September it is sweeter and suitable for dessert. It does not store well.

HARVEST TIME September to early October.

REGIONS WHERE GROWN All apple-growing regions.

GROWING TIPS A vigorous grower, this tree produces heavy crops. It develops a dense head that must be thinned annually to let in sun and air. 'Smokehouse' grows well in both clay and loam soils.

It exhibits some resistance to collar rot and is slightly susceptible to scab, cedar-apple rust, fire blight, and mildew. It is hardy in Zones 5 to 8.

—TB

'Sonata'

The cream-colored flesh of 'Sonata' is firm and finely grained with an excellent, sweet-tart to tart flavor somewhat similar to that of 'Golden Delicious'. The fruit is medium sized with a bright orangish-pink blush over a yellow background. Breeders in Germany and Poland worked for 18 years on this apple, a cross of 'Clivia' ('Cox's Orange Pippin' × 'Duchess of Oldenburg') and 'Golden Delicious'. Before it was given its current name, 'Sonata' was called 'Pinova' and then 'Corail'.

CULINARY USES This is an excellent dessert fruit and needs evaluation as a cooker. The fruit is best after a few months in storage.

HARVEST TIME Early to mid-October.

REGIONS WHERE GROWN Pacific Northwest and Michigan to the East Coast.

GROWING TIPS The tree of this variety has a spreading habit and is moderately vigorous at best. It grows well on M.9 and M.26 rootstocks. The tree blooms in midseason and will not pollinate 'Gala' or 'Jonagold'. Highly productive, it bears fruit on one-year-old shoots. Thin the fruits to eight inches apart. If the tree is grown in soil that's high in nitrogen, the fruits will lack color. 'Sonata' shows low susceptibility to apple scab and fire

When harvested in August, dense, chewy, and tender 'Smokehouse' is best used for cooking. Apples picked starting in September are sweeter and suitable for dessert.

blight, as well as to winter and spring frosts. The range of this new introduction is not proven, but 'Sonata' does well in the Pacific Northwest and should grow well in Zones 4 to 8. (It survived German and Polish winters to minus 13°F with no problems.)

—TS

'Spigold'

'Spigold' is a favorite among apple enthusiasts, who value its juicy crispness, fine texture, and excellent flavor. Its not an attractive apple, but it is delicious, with a rich and full taste that is high in sugars and acids. The fruits are large to very large, round, and sometimes irregular and often ribbed, with a pink- to red-striped blush over a yellowish-green undercolor. Skin and fruit are very fragile and bruise easily. Introduced in 1963, 'Spigold' originated at the New York Agricultural Experiment Station as a cross of 'Red Spy' and 'Golden Delicious', combining the best features of both parents. This farmers'-market favorite is found in many regions.

CULINARY USES This excellent dessert apple also cooks well, preserving its texture and flavor when baked or made into sauce. It is also an excellent cider or juice apple. It does not store well, developing a very greasy coating and turning slightly mealy within a few months.

HARVEST TIME Mid-autumn.

REGIONS WHERE GROWN Mountainous areas of the South and Southeast, up through the Midwest and Northeast.

GROWING TIPS While the fruits combine the best of their parents, the 'Spigold' tree has a tendency to combine their worst traits. It is slow to

A rich full taste high in sugars and acids has turned 'Spigold' into a favorite at farmers' markets in many regions.

mature into production, and when fruiting, it has a tenacious habit to bear biennially that is almost impossible to manage: It produces good crops one year and essentially none the following season, so growers must live with "on" and "off" years. 'Spigold' is very vigorous, forming a large round canopy, and does best on a dwarfing rootstock. It is triploid and not useful as a pollinator for other cultivars. The tree benefits from good pruning to improve structure and light penetration, which is critically important for flower formation. 'Spigold' requires 160 to 180 frost-free days from bloom until harvest, as well as a warm microclimate, since it is sensitive to frost. It is very susceptible to fire blight and is susceptible to apple scab and cedar-apple rust. The fruits are prone to the physiological disorder bitter pit when grown too vigorously or when the crop is light.

—CR

'Spokane Beauty'

This apple can grow very large—up to two pounds! Its flesh is white, crisp, and juicy, and its appealingly tart flavor resembling 'Gravenstein' has gained it quite a following among apple lovers. It tends to have a variable to lopsided shape with light green skin and carmine stripes. The apple reportedly made its first appearance outside Walla Walla, Washington, in the later half of the 19th century, from seeds planted by settler Stephen Maxson. 'Spokane Beauty' was awarded first prize at the Spokane Fruit Fair in 1895 and 1896, and in an entry of its 1913 catalog, the Oregon Nursery Company described it as follows: "Largest apple known, a prodigy for size; of extraordinary beauty...; flesh crisp, juicy, rich with a delicious, high flavor. Unsurpassed for cooking and drying; a very long keeper..." Despite these virtues, however, because of its size, 'Spokane Beauty' is not grown commercially.

CULINARY USES 'Spokane Beauty' is a good dessert apple; the tart flavor remains intact when the fruit is cooked or dried. Its large size is an advantage for culinary use. This apple stores well for up to three months.

HARVEST TIME Late September to mid-October in the Pacific Northwest.

REGIONS WHERE GROWN Pacific Northwest as a novelty apple.

GROWING TIPS Because 'Spokane Beauty' is a strong tip bearer, the limbs are long and weak and should be pruned accordingly. Grow this vigorous tree on M.9 to M.26 rootstock to control its size. 'Spokane Beauty' is rarely grown outside the Pacific Northwest, but its place of origin indicates that it can survive heat. It has little disease resistance but is only moderately susceptible to scab and powdery mildew. It is hardy in Zones 4 to 6.

—TS

'Stayman'

'Stayman' quickly gained popularity after it was discovered on the Kansas farm of Dr. J. Stayman in the mid-1800s. This 'Winesap' seedling spread from the Midwest into the South and through the Appalachian and Piedmont regions, and was widely grown at the turn of the 20th century. It is still popular today at roadside stands and farmers' markets. The yellow-white flesh is finely textured, juicy, and moderately acidic with a sprightly, winelike taste. The firm, somewhat crisp fruits are medium to large and round to slightly oblong. The thin, fragile skin will color with a light red stripe to crimson blush over a green to greenish-yellow undercolor. 'Stayman' is sometimes called 'Stayman Winesap'.

CULINARY USES 'Stayman' is a tasty dessert apple but is more commonly used for sauces and pies. It is good in cider blends, to which it gives a full, rich flavor that is more acidic than sweet. Fruits soften when picked overripe and are very prone to cracking if it rains during harvest. They can readily be stored for two to three months, but they soften and lose quality after that.

HARVEST TIME Mid-fall.

REGIONS WHERE GROWN Midwest, South, and throughout the Appalachian and Piedmont regions.

'Stayman' is popular for sauces and pies. Its winelike taste also makes it good in cider blends, to which it gives a full, rich flavor that is more acidic than sweet.

GROWING TIPS The tree is vigorous, producing a dense, leafy canopy that benefits from pruning to open it up. It does well on size-controlling rootstocks. 'Stayman' is triploid and so requires another tree that flowers at the same time as a pollinator; it cannot be used to pollinate other cultivars. It requires 165 to 175 frost-free days between bloom and harvest. 'Stayman' is moderately resistant to apple scab and cedar-apple rust but is susceptible to fire blight. The tree is prone to powdery mildew, which will cause a netted russeting of the fruit skin.

—CR

'Summer Champion'

This traditional southern apple has been grown extensively throughout the Southeast and Midwest for the past century. It ripens in midsummer, providing a nice break from other summer fruits, and is a harbinger of fall. The light yellow, crisp, juicy, and moderately acidic flesh develops a well-balanced flavor during cooler summers. It has a good "old-time" apple flavor that's reminiscent of apple cider. Fruits are medium sized, round to slightly conical, and have pink to red stripes over a yellow-green undercolor. There is often russeting in the stem cavity, and powdery mildew may cause a netted russet over some of the fruit. The apple originated as a chance seedling in Arkansas in 1897 and was sold for decades by Stark Bro's Nursery.

CULINARY USES 'Summer Champion' can be eaten fresh; it also makes good sauce and apple butter. Fruits become soft if overripe or stored for more than a few weeks. Eat or process them immediately.

HARVEST TIME This summer apple ripens around the same time as peaches. The fruits may ripen over a two-week period.

REGIONS WHERE GROWN Throughout the South and into the Midwest.

GROWING TIPS An advantage of early-season apples—other than having fresh fruit in midsummer—is that the trees require very little care and no sprays or pesticides for pests that emerge after the fruit harvest. Be sure to continue to water, though. This tree requires only 90 to 100 frost-free days from bloom until harvest (about half the "apple season" of other cultivars). The fruits can withstand the heat and intense sun of southern regions but also do well in climates with cooler summers. The moderately vigorous tree does well on a dwarfing rootstock and bears a crop annually. Thin the fruit aggressively to improve fruit size. 'Summer Champion' may be susceptible to apple scab and is moderately susceptible to cedar-apple rust.

—CR

'Summer Rambo'

The pale greenish-yellow skin of 'Summer Rambo' is blushed pale red, streaked carmine, and scattered with russet patches. Its flesh is yellowish, fine-grained, juicy, and firm—a bite from the apple makes a crunching sound. The fruit has a mildly acidic, slightly sweet flavor that turns winelike when it is well ripened. Large and flattish, it is lightly ribbed on the body and prominently ribbed at the eye. 'Summer Rambo' was grown as early as 1767 in colonial America and is thought to have originated in the town of Rambure, near Abbeville in northern France, where it was recorded in 1535. 'Summer Rambo',

Often picked in mid-July before they have fully ripened and sold simply as green cooking apples, 'Summer Rambo' fruits are very desirable for fresh eating when allowed to mature on the tree.

also called 'Lorraine', 'Summer Rambour', and 'Rambour Franc' in France, is often confused with the distinct variety 'Rambo'. There also is a red cultivar called 'Redsumbo'.

CULINARY USES The apples are often picked in mid-July and sold in country stores and farmers' markets as green cooking apples. When allowed to mature on the tree, this variety is a highly desirable dessert fruit.

HARVEST TIME Early August, but it is often picked in July in the green stage for culinary use.

REGIONS WHERE GROWN Not only is this grandfather of apples cultivated in all apple-growing regions of North America, it is grown in temperate zones throughout the world.

GROWING TIPS One of the most dependable of all apple varieties, the vigorous tree bears early, annually, and heavily and will produce high-quality apples with good fruit-tree culture. On standard rootstock the tree grows very large. It is fairly resistant to the major apple diseases and is hardy in Zones 5 to 8.

—TB

'Williams' Pride'

This variety has unusually good flavor and texture for a summer apple. Medium sized and somewhat conical, the apples are deep red over a green

apple does well in a range of climates and is suitable for Zones 5 to 7.

—*IM*

background that breaks to yellow as they ripen. The yellow flesh is granular, crisp, and mildly acidic, with occasional streaks of red below the skin. This is another in the series of disease-resistant apples developed by the fruit-breeding program at Purdue/Rutgers/Illinois universities. (It is PRI1018-101 crossed with NJ50 and was introduced in 1988.)

CULINARY USES 'Williams' Pride' is excellent for pies, ciders, and fresh eating. It will keep for a month or so.

HARVEST TIME 'Williams' Pride' ripens over several weeks during early to mid-August.

REGIONS WHERE GROWN This relatively new variety is grown mostly in the Mid-Atlantic region.

GROWING TIPS This is a vigorous and productive tree; its lateral branches are flexible and droop when loaded with ripe apples, so the trees eventually begin to sprawl. Best suited to dwarf or semidwarf rootstocks, this variety deserves a place in the home garden for its disease resistance, productivity, early ripening, and good-quality fruit. 'Williams' Pride' is immune to scab and cedar-apple rust and resistant to fire blight and powdery mildew. This

'Winesap'

This variety's winelike flavor and acidity, its crisp, firm flesh, very long-term storage potential, and wide climatic adaptation made it one of the most popular apples in the early 1900s. 'Winesap' originated as a chance seedling in New Jersey around 1817. It produces a medium to large, dark red apple with firm, yellow flesh. 'Winesap' is less widely grown than it once was (it was supplanted by 'Red Delicious' in many commercial orchards) and is often confused with its many seedling offsprings, such as 'Stayman Winesap', 'Paragon Winesap', and others. This apple's reputation was further muddied by nurseries that promoted more than a dozen "improved" strains of 'Winesap' that often lacked the eating quality of the original. Although it is no longer a main variety in commercial orchards, 'Winesap' is highly esteemed by apple aficionados and is still popular regionally in farmers' markets.

CULINARY USES Excellent for all uses and highly valued for cider blends. It can be stored for more than six months.

HARVEST TIME Late October in the Northeast and somewhat earlier in warmer regions.

A fruit that keeps apple aficionados company throughout the winter, 'Winesap' is especially prized for cider blends.

Typically grown for applesauce and picked a bit green, 'Yellow Transparent' is one of the earliest summer apples. It does not store well and needs to be eaten or processed quickly after harvest.

REGIONS WHERE GROWN Once widely grown in the Northwest, 'Winesap' is now grown mostly in Virginia, North Carolina, Washington, and in limited plantings elsewhere.

GROWING TIPS 'Winesap' is moderately vigorous and well suited to semidwarf rootstocks. It has infertile pollen, so it will not cross-pollinate other varieties. When grown in fertile, well-drained soils, the tree reliably produces a good crop annually. 'Winesap' has a long and distinguished history in America and deserves consideration by home garden-

ers who want a sweet and tart juicy apple. It is resistant to cedar-apple rust but susceptible to other apple diseases. It is suited to areas with hot summers in Zones 5 to 8.

—*IM*

'Yellow Transparent'

This immigrant from Russia is among the earliest-ripening summer apples and is sold in local and roadside markets throughout the Southeast and Midwest. Introduced by the United States Department of Agriculture as a winter-hardy variety in 1870, it has become a traditional southern countryside apple over the years. The fruit is juicy and somewhat crisp, with a pleasant, moderately acidic flavor. The flesh is clear white to light yellow, and the skin is yellow to whitish yellow and so thin as to be almost transparent, hence the name. The medium to large fruits are slightly oblong and bruise easily. Since 'Yellow Transparent' is typically picked a bit green, it is thought of as a tart apple. It is also called 'Russian Transparent', 'June Transparent', or 'Early Transparent'.

CULINARY USES Not bad as a dessert apple, it is typically grown to make a fresh-flavored applesauce with good color. The fruits bake and fry well, too. They ripen unevenly and the flesh becomes mealy and dry when overripe, getting sweeter along the way. 'Yellow Transparent' does not store well and so must be eaten or processed quickly after harvest.

HARVEST TIME June to July.

REGIONS WHERE GROWN The South, Midwest, and other apple-growing regions.

GROWING TIPS 'Yellow Transparent' is very prolific and tends to set heavy crops annually. The tree is precocious, bearing fruit relatively young. It is not very vigorous and benefits from annual pruning to encourage the development of new fruiting wood. The tree tends to bloom relatively early and may be susceptible to frost. The fruits are borne on sturdy, spurry branches; thin them to achieve good fruit size. 'Yellow Transparent' is among the earliest apples, ripening 75 to 90 days after bloom. It has done well in cold northern regions with very short summers. It is very winter hardy, probably down to Zone 4. It is resistant to both cedar-apple rust and apple scab. It is susceptible to fire blight, and powdery mildew will affect shoots and cause russeting on the otherwise smooth fruit skin.

—CR

The ABCs of Growing Apples at Home

Ed Fackler

Having been cultivated for several thousand years, apples are among the most widely planted fruits in the world—and with good reason. If you choose varieties suited to your particular climate and growing conditions, you can grow these wonderful treats in most temperate zones.

North America comprises three apple growing zones. Alaska, Canada, and the upper quarter of the contiguous states make up the coldest zone suitable for apple cultivation. Gardeners in this region grow varieties that can produce a crop within a relatively short growing season and are hardy enough to withstand harsh winter temperatures.

The central apple-growing region is bounded on the north by an imaginary line running from Seattle, Washington, via Chicago, Illinois, to Portland, Maine. The southern boundary of this section runs from San Francisco, California, via Tulsa, Oklahoma, to Richmond, Virginia. Growers in this region generally have to contend with a host of pests, but otherwise they can grow most any apple variety.

The southern apple region includes everything south of the San Francisco-Tulsa-Richmond line. Apples suitable to the climate in this region must be able to tolerate extreme heat when the fruit is ripening.

As the seedlings usually bear only a glancing resemblance to their parent tree, practically all apples, including those in the basket, come from trees that have been cloned, or propagated vegetatively.

Connecting Fruits and Roots

All apple trees available in nurseries are propagated by grafting a scion—a dormant shoot of a selected variety—onto the rootstock of a different variety. The scion grows into the upper, fruiting part of the tree. The rootstock forms the roots and lower trunk of the tree. The exact same thing can be accomplished by budding, but it requires a two-year process and is a bit more complex. Grafting enables growers to combine desirable fruit and root characteristics from two different trees with a predictable result, with the scion determining the properties of the fruit and the rootstock determining some important properties of the tree. Propagated vegetatively, the scion produces fruit that is exactly the same as that of its parent. Apples from a 'McIntosh' scion are identical to those of the tree that the scion was taken from. The rootstock influences the ultimate size of the tree and can enhance the tree's drought tolerance, productivity, soil-borne pest resistance, or the age at which the tree begins to produce fruit. The rootstock has little effect on the fruit itself, so a 'McIntosh' apple tastes and looks the same no matter what type of rootstock it has been grown on. (For more on the practical aspects of grafting, see "A Grafting Primer," page 92.)

This is good news for apple growers who can buy the varieties they would like to cultivate on the rootstocks that best fit their needs. An overwhelming number of today's common apple rootstocks are clonally reproduced in stool beds, a system in which mother plants are established and forced to sprout from roots; these sprouts are harvested each winter and used as rootstocks in the subsequent grafting and budding to produce new trees. Other standard rootstocks are grown from seed. Rootstocks fall into one of four categories: standard, semidwarf, dwarf, and super- or mini-dwarf. Scions grafted onto vigorous or standard rootstock grow into full-sized, or slightly smaller than full-sized, trees, reaching about 15 to 20 feet in height. The most common standard rootstock is MM111 (named after the East Malling Research Station in England, where many of the early rootstocks were developed). Semidwarf rootstocks produce trees that are 50 to 70 percent the size of full-sized trees, and most produce fruit several years earlier than trees grown on standard rootstocks. It is not fully understood why trees grown on dwarfing stocks are quicker to bear than those grown on so-called vigorous, or standard-size, rootstocks. One common theory is that the dwarf stocks induce fruit-spur hormones sooner and therefore, these trees

continues on page 94

The most common technique for propagating apples vegetatively is dormant-wood grafting, in which the dormant shoot of one variety is combined with the rootstock of another variety. In the tree pictured here, a shoot of 'Freedom' was grafted onto a dwarfing rootstock to produce a small tree.

A Grafting Primer

Tom Burford

Occasionally, out of thousands and thousands of worthless—from the apple eater's point of view—seedlings produced by every apple tree, a variety that tastes sublime will appear. These rare occurrences have given rise to many of the classic varieties described on pages 29 to 87. To ensure that worthy varieties endure, apple propagators take small cuttings, called scions, from the fruit-bearing parts of a tree that produces desirable fruit and graft them to rootstocks to create new trees.

Grafting requires manual dexterity and experience, but it is an agricultural skill home gardeners can master with practice. Sometimes it may even be the only way to preserve an old variety discovered in an abandoned orchard. Before you set out, purchase rootstocks from a nursery. (For more on rootstocks, see pages 90 and 109.)

There are two basic methods of grafting: Dormant-wood grafting (whip and tongue grafting or cleft and saddle grafting) is performed in February and March with dormant buds taken from storage (see below). Live-wood grafting (shield, or "T" grafting, or chip grafting) is done in June or late August using buds taken from an actively growing tree.

Whip and tongue grafting is one of the most popular techniques. Success rates depend on timing, the sharpness of the grafting knife, the quality of scion wood and rootstock, and how well the cambium—the portion of the tree that produces new growth—of each piece contacts the cambium of the other piece.

WHIP AND TONGUE GRAFTING

In January or February, cut six- or eight-inch long sections from a branch that formed the previous season from the apple variety you wish to propagate. Use only buds from growth of the previous season. Label and store the branch sections, or scions, in a plastic bag in the refrigerator until late February or March, the time for dormant-wood grafting.

STEP ONE Take the rootstock and cut the stem off a few inches above the topmost roots. With a very sharp, thin-bladed knife, make a diagonal cut one half to one inch long through the stem toward the lower tip of the rootstock.

STEP TWO To make the tongue cut, slice into the wood about one third inch of the distance from the top of the flat cut surface and draw the knife downward parallel to the back of the stem most of the way to the bottom of the exposed flat surface. The tongue cut will mechanically bind the parts and maximize cambium contact.

STEP THREE Select the variety to graft from the scion wood stored in the refrigerator, choosing one with a diameter as close as possible to that of the rootstock. Make the same two cuts as above on the scion wood, making sure that the buds point upward when attached. After the scion wood is prepared, prune off all but two or three buds.

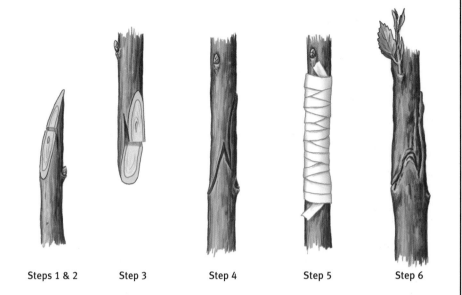

Steps 1 & 2   Step 3   Step 4   Step 5   Step 6

STEP FOUR Bring the two pieces together by sliding the cut of the scion tongue over the cut of the rootstock tongue, making sure that the cambium cells (evident as a thin, light green line around the perimeter of the cut surfaces) are touching each other.

If the scion piece is smaller than the rootstock, align the scion along one side of the rootstock. If there is no match of cambium cells from the two pieces, the graft will fail.

STEP FIVE Wrap the union with adhesive-like grafting tape, freezer tape (found in most supermarkets), or even black electrician's tape to keep the moisture inside from drying up and outside moisture from entering the union. (You will have to carefully slit electrician's tape as the plant grows to allow for expansion. Freezer tape will deteriorate as the plant grows.)

Cover the top of the scion piece to prevent moisture loss. Grafting sealants are available, but you can also use white glue or petroleum jelly.

STEP SIX Label the new tree and put the entire plant in a plastic bag for a few weeks, storing it at average room temperature out of the sun. Once the cambium tissues of the scion and rootstock unite, the buds will begin to swell, and it's time to remove the bag.

When the outside temperature no longer dips below freezing, plant the young tree in a nursery row in the garden or in a pot. With good care, the tree will grow four or five feet in its first year, and will be ready for transplanting to its permanent site the following spring.

Attach a permanent label to each new tree, record it in a log book, and fence or cage the tree against damage by varmints.

Most apple trees cannot pollinate themselves. To assure good cross-pollination, several varieties need to be planted in proximity to each other.

continued from page 90

start flowering and fruiting sooner. Furthermore, the earlier fruiting in itself has a dwarfing influence on the tree. Common semidwarf rootstocks include M7, which produces a tree half the size of a standard tree, and MM106, which produces a slightly larger tree than M7. Dwarf, or full-dwarf, rootstocks are excellent for gardeners with limited space. They produce trees that grow from eight to ten feet tall, begin to bear in their second or third year, and require some type of permanent support. Among those commonly used are M9 and B9 (Bud9). Even better for backyard apple growers are super- or mini-dwarf trees. These trees almost never exceed six feet in height. Super-dwarf trees almost always begin fruiting in the second year after planting and, like dwarf apple trees, they require lifelong support. They are most commonly grafted to M27 or P22 rootstocks. (To find out more about growing apples in small spaces, see "Planting an Apple Hedge," page 107.)

Choosing Varieties

With as many opinions about apple culture as there are people growing apples, determining which varieties will work best in your situation can be a daunting task. Not every apple will do well in all parts of the country. 'Ben Davis' won't grow in the North because the growing season is too short; 'Northern Spy' won't grow in the South because the weather is too hot. Be mindful of this North-South distinction and choose accordingly. You may want to seek out the advice of local orchardists. Their experience can be a great help in choosing varieties that will do well in your area. A pollination chart (found in nursery catalogs and books on apple culture) is another gold mine of information: It will tell you which trees need pollen, which ones provide pollen, and which ones are self-fertile. These charts also take into account how bloom times of different varieties overlap, especially important information to know when planting a mix of early and late varieties. Do your homework, and ask plenty of questions. There's one pollination trick that always seems to work: Include a 'Grimes Golden', 'Golden Delicious', or 'Winter Banana' in your planting. These varieties are known as reliable pollinators, and their midseason bloom time overlaps with just about any tree you could name.

Planting Apple Trees

How and where you plant apple trees are crucial factors that will influence their longevity and productivity. Begin by selecting a site that receives at least six hours of direct sunlight each day during the growing season. Then take a soil sample and have it analyzed by a reputable lab. A soil analysis will tell you if the soil meets the requirements for apple cultivation, and if it doesn't, the lab's report will include recommendations for possible soil amendments. Although apples require moderate amounts of all nutrients, they are heavy consumers of calcium, and getting adequate quantities of it to the fruit can be difficult. Most effective are pelletized or encapsulated forms of calcium, which are now commonly available and should be applied immediately after planting and again after the first year in which the tree bears fruit, if indeed the apples exhibit signs of calcium deficiency. After a year in which your trees have borne a heavy crop load, which can deplete them, apply a fertilizer that's high in potassium (such as 10-10-30) in late November or very early spring at around three to five pounds per bearing tree applied at the drip line. If you prefer, you can also apply bone meal, blood meal, and rock phosphate.

Plant apple trees as early in spring as possible before soil temperatures rise to 55°F, which means early April in most apple-growing regions. Most apples are not self-fertile—they are incapable of pollinating themselves—so you need to plant at least two different varieties for cross-pollination. You can also provide for pollination by

When choosing different apple varieties for your yard, be sure to orchestrate for overlapping bloom times, especially important when mixing early- and late-flowering varieties.

planting a crabapple nearby or placing a bouquet of apple blooms from another variety close to your tree while it's in bloom. Almost all varieties are "cross-compatible," or able to pollinate each other, but make sure that the trees you choose bloom at about the same time in spring and that neither is a triploid, a tree that has an extra set of chromosomes and produces sterile pollen. A good apple reference book, nursery, or your local cooperative extension service can help you sort this out.

Planting depth is critical with most dwarfing trees. Set the plants so that the graft union is about two inches above the soil level. If the union is below ground, the scion will root, and the dwarfing effect will be lost. If the union is more than three inches out of the ground, too much of the root shank will be exposed, which may cause other problems, such as an increased chance of winter injury, breakage—many dwarf rootstocks are very brittle—and aerial rooting, or burr knots, a host for borers.

Training Young Dwarf Apple Trees

Most dwarf (also known as full dwarf) and super-dwarf trees have relatively small and brittle root systems and require some sort of support throughout their lives. Use two-inch by two-inch by eight-foot stakes for individual tree support or a three- to four-wire trellis (similar to a grape trellis) to support the trees, or plant them along a boundary fence. Secure the fruiting limbs loosely to the support to create almost any artful form you desire.

Mulch newly planted trees heavily with organic matter such as leaves, straw, or wood chips. Keep the mulch a couple of inches away from the trunks to discourage rotting and field mouse damage at the bases. Remove the mulch during winter months to keep mice from sheltering in it and dining on tree bark. And make sure your trees receive an adequate supply of water, especially during their first, critical season in the ground.

Thinning Apples

Apple trees often set more fruit than can ripen to a desirable size. To increase the size and flavor of the fruits you harvest, you must thin the fruit on your trees annually. Fruit thinning also reduces many apple varieties' tendency to fruit biennially, which means they bear close to no fruit every other year. Since overloaded limbs can break off, thinning the fruit also helps you maintain a good tree form.

Begin thinning right after flowering, when little apples become visible. Remove all but one fruit per cluster, or spur, and remove entire clusters as needed to keep them no closer than eight inches apart. The center apple of a cluster is usually the largest apple and the best one to keep, unless it is blemished—if it is, select another apple.

Be sure to remove the apples you thin and any that may have fallen to the ground to a hot compost pile, or dispose of them in the garbage. These tiny fruits may already be harboring pest larvae and diseases.

continues on page 102

Right after flowering, when little apples become visible, remove all but one fruit from each cluster. Remove the entire cluster if it is closer than eight inches from the next one. Be sure to remove the apples you thin and any that may have fallen to the ground to a hot compost pile, or dispose of them in the garbage. The tiny fruits may already be harboring pest larvae and diseases.

Pruning Young and Mature Apple Trees

More art than science, pruning is a skill you will pick up over time. A regular annual pruning program is far better for your tree—and easier for you—than one done every few years or even every other year. Do most of your pruning in winter when the tree is dormant. The most important pruning goal is assuring that sufficient sunlight, at least six hours per day, reaches the maximum number of leaves. Keep this aim in mind when pruning mature trees or when training young trees to develop good structure.

Before you get started, inventory your tools and be sure to keep the proper equipment handy. Use hand pruners to cut branches up to a half inch in diameter; use loppers for limbs up to three quarters of an inch in diameter; use a pruning saw for larger cuts. Be certain that all the cutting tools are sharp.

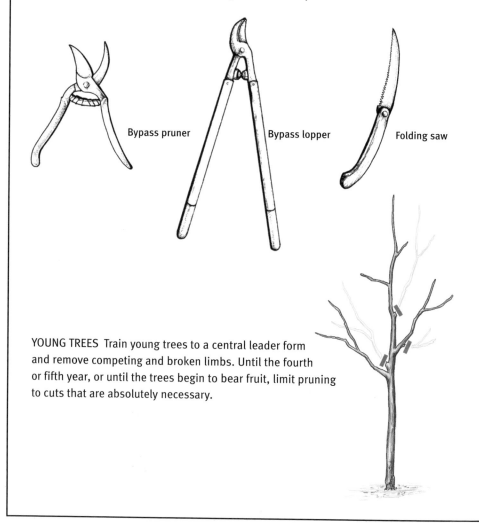

Bypass pruner   Bypass lopper   Folding saw

YOUNG TREES Train young trees to a central leader form and remove competing and broken limbs. Until the fourth or fifth year, or until the trees begin to bear fruit, limit pruning to cuts that are absolutely necessary.

FOURTH OR FIFTH YEAR Select the scaffold limbs, which will be permanent. Space the scaffold limbs about 12 to 18 inches apart, up and down the trunk. Spread or gently pull them until they are nearly parallel to the ground. Attach the limbs with twine to stakes, the support structure that's already in place, or spread them with spreaders made for this purpose. Do this only on a very hot day in late spring or early summer, when the temperature is at least 80°F. At this time the tree's wood is more flexible than on colder days.

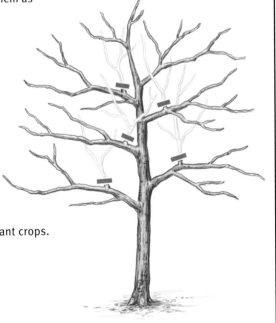

FOLLOWING YEARS Within a few years, your apple trees will start producing a crop, bearing their fruits on short growths called spurs. These are larger than vegetative buds and generally arise on the outer thirds of the scaffold limbs. They become overcrowded after a few years and must be thinned out to invigorate the tree and to space fruits properly. Once the trees are in heavy production (three years for super- or mini-dwarf trees, five to six years for semidwarf, and seven to eight years for standard), prune them as needed to open up the canopy to light and air circulation. The best way to do this is to remove entire branches. Take out shaded branches or those that shade lower branches and those that are competing with others nearby for space around the trunk. Always remember, the goal is to get plenty of light to the leaves, the tree's all-important solar collectors that allow it to gather the energy needed to grow tasty and abundant crops.

Restoring a Derelict Apple Tree

Tom Burford

If you have inherited a long-neglected apple tree, you have a stark choice: Removing the old tree and planting a new one or restoring the old tree, which takes considerable time and energy. When deciding whether or not to restore, consider the three main objectives of the project: enhancing your garden landscape, preserving a tree for sentimental or historical reasons, and developing a tree that will produce quality fruit of a variety that you cherish. If your objective is solely fruit production, planting a new apple tree is the logical choice, provided the variety is readily available.

If you determine that the elderly tree is worth preserving, establish a restoration program that stretches over three to five years, with the goal to bring the tree back to good health and productivity. When you first get out pruners, loppers, and saws, take a look at what grows in the tree's immediate surroundings, remove any competitors for sunlight and nutrients, and clear all vegetation from beneath the tree.

As you plan a renovation strategy for your tree, keep these goals in mind. You should be aiming to:

Control tree size and vigor by proper pruning and a fertilization program.

Produce fruit of good quality and large size by ensuring good pollination, judicious fruit thinning, and a spray program.

Encourage the production of blossoms for fruiting by pruning annually to promote the production of new wood.

Distribute fruiting wood along the branches by pruning during the dormant period as well as removing water sprouts during the summer months.

Minimize limb breakage by developing scaffold limbs with wide branch unions.

Facilitate harvesting by pruning to keep the canopy low and spacing limbs so that they spiral up the trunk of the tree.

Do most of the pruning in winter when the tree is dormant. To remove branches that are larger than three quarters of an inch in diameter, cut just outside the branch collar. Cut all smaller branches flush with the stem from which they emerge, making sure not to leave stubs, which can harbor diseases and insects. Do not remove massive amounts of growth in any single year, as this will stimulate the production of excess vegetation. Instead, remove a quarter to a third of live growth each year. Be sure to prune out entire limbs rather than snip the ends off branches. Snipping will stimulate unwanted vegetative growth along the branches.

Strategies for a Three- to Five-Year Restoration Program

Derelict apple trees can be dangerous. Limbs may appear to be solid and then break suddenly under the weight of a person. Working from a sturdy ladder is much safer than standing in the tree. Teaming up with a partner who can steady the ladder provides extra safety.

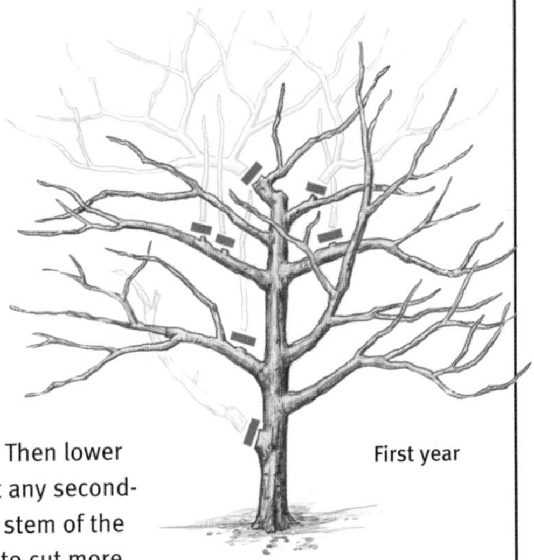

FIRST YEAR Start by removing dead limbs, water sprouts, and crossed limbs. Then lower some of the top of the tree by cutting out any secondary main stems and shortening the main stem of the tree by three or four feet. Remember not to cut more than one quarter to one third live wood, and don't apply nitrogen fertilizer in the first year.

First year

SECOND AND THIRD YEARS Remove any new water sprouts and continue to remove crossed limbs and any limbs that grow directly above another limb.

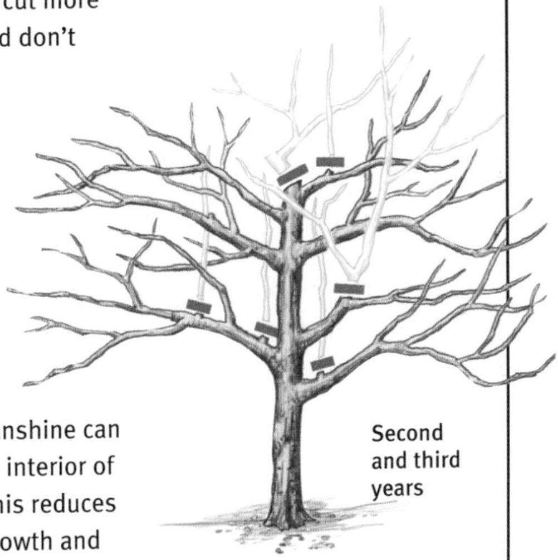

FOLLOWING YEARS Develop a regular late-winter pruning schedule with the goal of keeping the canopy open so that sunshine can penetrate and air can circulate through the interior of the tree. This reduces fungal growth and enhances the quality of the fruit. When evaluating new branches, look for strong branch unions and eliminate any limbs with narrow crotch angles while they are still young.

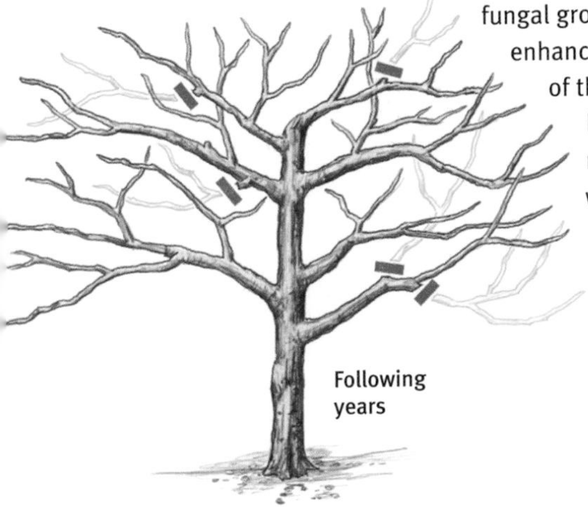

Second and third years

Following years

Varieties suitable for storage can usually be kept for several months in a place where temperatures remain between 30°F and 40°F and humidity is high enough to prevent desiccation.

continued from page 97

Harvesting and Storing Apples

The most reliable indicator of your fruit's ripeness—other than your taste buds—is the change in its green undercolor, or ground color, from a grass green to a softer yellow green. You can also judge your fruit's readiness for harvest by observing changes in seed-coat color. When immature, apple seed coats are creamy white. As the fruit matures they darken to deep brown.

Many apple varieties can be stored for many months under the right conditions. For long-term storage, select fruits that are totally free of blemishes and not overly ripe. Store them between 30°F and 40°F, with enough humidity to prevent them from drying out. Cool the apples to the storage temperature quickly to prevent further ripening. Wrap them in plastic bags or place them in covered containers with a few holes for air circulation, and add a few drops of water to keep the air inside moist.

Apple varieties that hold up exceedingly well in long-term storage (even in a basement) include 'GoldRush', 'Sundance', 'Fuji', and 'Granny Smith'. All keep for four months or more in an unheated basement. Some antique apples even require storage:

'Arkansas Black' is so hard at harvest time that it is nearly inedible, but it mellows after several months in storage, and 'Newtown Pippin' does not attain its renowned flavor until it's been in storage for two or three months.

Managing Insect Pests and Diseases

Apple trees are hosts to many insect and disease pests, which can prevent them from producing good fruit. The list of potential insect pests is long, but not all pests are active in all regions. Codling moth and aphids, for example, are particularly problematic on the West Coast. East of the Rockies, major insect pests include plum curculio, codling moth, aphids, and, in more northern regions, apple maggot. A local nursery or cooperative extension office can tell you which pests are problems in your area and how to respond.

Bacterial and fungal diseases that attack apples include apple scab, cedar-apple rust, and powdery mildew, as well as fire blight, a bacterial infection that causes leaves and stems to look as if they have been blackened by fire. (Control fire blight by planting resistant apple varieties, pruning off diseased stems, and preventing overly lush growth, which is very susceptible to the disease.) The easiest way to deal with apple diseases is prevention: Find out which diseases are prevalent in your area and plant varieties that are resistant to them.

Top: Apple maggots have wreaked havoc on these apples. To find out which pests are active in your area and how to respond, contact your local cooperative extension or a nursery.

Bottom: Apple leaves damaged by cedar-apple rust, one of the many diseases that attack apples.

Many excellent new apple varieties have been bred for resistance to one or more of the serious apple diseases. These include 'Enterprise', page 42, 'GoldRush', page 49, 'Liberty', page 63, and 'Williams' Pride', page 83.

Rather than attempting to control insect pests and diseases with toxic chemicals, it's much safer for you, your family, and the environment to follow organic practices. By pruning your tree to allow maximum air movement and let sunlight in, you can do a lot to maintain its health and keep diseases and pests at bay. In addition, a fine-tuned combination of two organic agents—Surround, a kaolin clay powder that deters insect pests if sprayed at the proper time, and sulphur, a fungicide that is applied at specific intervals—have proven successful. The application times are based on specific periods each growing season, notably the "tight-cluster" stage (when blooms are clustered but not showing any pink), "pink" stage (when blooms are showing pink color but are not yet open), "petal-fall" stage (when 90 percent of the petals have fallen), and again at two-week intervals after petal fall.

Experimental trials of many new organic controls of apple pests are currently under way. Contact your local cooperative extension agent for a list of apple pests in your area and appropriate controls.

Disease-Resistant Apples

Variety	Season of Maturity	Uses	Disease Resistance				
			Scab	CAR	MW	FB	SR
'Pristine'	Early to mid-July	F, C, J	VR	MR	R	S	VR
'Williams' Pride'	Early to mid-July	F, C, J, D	VR	R	R	R	VR
'Redfree'	Late July	F, J, D	VR	R	R	R	R
'Pixie Crunch'	Late August	F, J,	VR	?	MR	MR	MR
'Novamac'	Early September	F, C, J	VR	R	MR	MR	S
'Liberty'	Early September	F, J	VR	R	R	R	S
'Enterprise'	Late September	F, J, C	VR	R	R	VR	S
'Sundance'	Late September	F, J, D	VR	R	MR	MR	S
'Nova Easygro'	Late September	F, J	VR	?	S	MR	S
'Florina'	Early October	F, J	VR	R	MR	MR	S
'NovaSpy'	Early October	F, C, J	VR	S	?	MR	S
'GoldRush'	Mid-October	F, C, J, D	VR	S	R	MR	S

KEY TO ABBREVIATIONS

USES F: Fresh eating; C: Culinary (pies, tarts, sauce); J: Juice; D: Drying

DISEASES CAR: Cedar-apple rust; MW: Mildew; FB: Fire blight; SR: Summer rots

DISEASE RATINGS VR: Very resistant (no sprays required); R: Resistant (generally no sprays required); MR: Tolerant; S: Susceptible; ?: Resistance not known

Apple growers in the northernmost range must also protect their trees against sun scald, damage caused in winter when snow reflects sunlight onto the trunk. The southwest side of the trunk can be radically warmed by the heat, and very cold nighttime temperatures can cause the trunk to split. Apply a protective paint (white latex) on the southwest side of the tree from the ground up to a height of 24 inches. The white paint reflects the sunlight away from the tree, moderating trunk temperatures.

Bagging Fruits to Control Pests and Diseases

Ted Swensen

A relatively new approach to pest and disease control is to protect fruits with tinted paper bags. Besides blocking pests, the bags also block sunlight, giving the apples a paler, more delicate finish. Bagging also enhances the sugar content of apples. This is much safer than the application of chemical pesticides, which is tricky, requiring perfect timing, and also quite toxic, releasing poisons into the environment. You can quit spraying altogether and instead protect apples from their attackers by enclosing the fruit in bags when they are still very young. Leave the apples in the bags until just before harvest, and they'll be safe from almost all the pests and diseases that damage fruits and make them unsightly.

Bags designed specifically for apple bagging are available, but No. 4–size brown and white bags work just as well. White bags allow the fruit to color inside the bag, but the ones I've used are not very weather resistant and come unglued. Bagged in brown paper, the fruits will not color, but the bags are hold up better. You can get

Enclosed in bags while they are still small, apples are protected against pests and diseases without spraying. The bags are removed several weeks before harvest to allow the apples to color.

your fruit to color by removing the bags two to three weeks before harvest. Amazingly, the apples will develop as much or more color as those exposed all season.

I bag fruit when it's one half to three quarters of an inch in diameter, usually 35 to 40 days after the blossoms drop. This is a convenient time because I'm already working on my trees then, thinning the clusters to a single fruit. For the bagging to be effective, you must complete the job before the pests arrive to infest your fruit. You can use pheromone traps to alert you when the pests start showing up, then you'll need to hustle. Traps are available for most of the universal apple pests: codling moth, apple maggot, and leaf rollers.

Some people use twist ties to secure the bags, but since most of my fingers act as thumbs, I use a stapler. Before bagging, staple each bag in four places: Starting at one edge, staple near the edge and near the small dip at the top center of the bag. Then apply two staples at the other edge and near the small dip in the bag. Leave an opening large enough at the dip to open the bag and slip it over the developing fruit. Once the fruit is inside the bag, slide the fruit stem over to one side and staple. Take care not to damage the stem of the fruit, which will cause it to drop.

When you get the hang of it, you can bag three or four apples a minute. About a hundred apples is a reasonable number to let develop on a mature dwarf tree. Remove all unbagged apples to prevent pest populations from increasing. That's all you need to do. Your fruit is now well protected from both diseases and insects.

Deer, Rabbit, and Mouse Control

Deer love the foliage, flowers, and fruit of apple trees, and they can destroy a young apple tree in one night. Short of a prohibitive fence eight feet tall, there is little you can do. For short-term protection, you can spray your trees every ten days or so with a substance that makes the foliage unpalatable to deer (the active ingredient is usually the fungicide Thiram).

Rabbits simply love to chew the bark off young apple trees during the winter months. You can keep them away by shielding the lower part of the trees with a 20-inch-high protector—a white plastic spiral, a low fence, or even a circular cardboard enclosure—which should be in place by November and removed by mid-May. Field mice and voles can also severely damage the lower tree trunks. They set up a motel under a layer of mulch during the winter months and make forays from there to the trees. You can prevent small rodent damage by keeping an 18-inch circle around the trunks clear of mulch in winter.

Super-dwarf apple trees can be planted closely together to fit an entire orchard into a very small space.

Planting an Apple Hedge: An Orchard for Small Spaces

Tim Hensley

In our backyard orchard, my wife and I grow 24 varieties of apples. Our house is sited on a 50- by 150-foot city lot, and our orchard occupies roughly 120 square feet—less than half the area gobbled by a single mature semidwarf tree. We can grow this many trees because we have planted them as a kind of informal espalier, or dwarf apple hedge. And because we've chosen varieties that ripen over the entire harvest season, we enjoy our own apples from June to November.

An apple hedge invites interaction, so locate it conveniently, in a spot where it will thrive. We planted ours in a terraced bed that runs along the upper edge of our back-yard. The site gets plenty of sunlight; it is elevated sufficiently for good airflow; and it is visible from our kitchen window so we can keep an eye out for apple-pecking jays and starlings during the harvest season. One drawback of our site is its west-facing slope: Apples on a south or west face tend to bloom early, which makes them susceptible to late frosts. They also tend to drop fruit during extended periods of hot,

An attractive way to grow apples in a tight space, an espalier is just as easy to maintain as any other apple hedge.

dry weather. It's best to plant apple trees on a north or east-facing slope, but it's okay to bend the rule if your home garden will not allow it.

Dwarf trees are notoriously prone to uprooting under the weight of a heavy crop, so it's essential to grow them on a support structure, and there are a number of ways to do it. You can grow your trees against a fence—almost any kind will do: board, rail, even chain link; you can plant them next to a building; or you can provide a free-standing support in the form of a trellis, which is what we opted for. We created our trellis using four- by four-inch posts spaced ten feet apart and three strands of heavy-gauge galvanized wire. I secured the galvanized wires to the posts with regular fencing staples, but it didn't take long for some of the wires to begin to work loose. In time, I reworked most of the stapled wires by securing them to eyebolts and adding a turn-buckle to allow for periodic tightening. If you plan to install more than 30 trees, you might check out some of the commercial trellis systems now available. Such hardware can be pricey, but it is relatively easy to install and made to last for many years.

SPACING ESPALIERED TREES

The standard for high-density commercial plantings is to allow five or six feet between trees, but we spaced our trees two feet apart because we wanted to grow lots of different apples in a very small space. On the most dwarfing rootstocks, super- or mini-dwarfs, trees may be planted as close as one foot apart.

Such spacing necessitates pruning to a very specific form. We chose what might be called an oblique fan. Like any espalier, it is easy to maintain because it is pruned to two dimensions, and it is a little more artistic than a simple straight-up planting. Other espalier forms to consider for an apple hedge include the oblique cordon, the Belgian fence, and the double-U palmate.

The quantity of fruit produced by a single dwarf tree is quite small (about 1½ bushels or less). So if you're interested in putting away lots of apple preserves, you'll need to plant several trees of the same variety to get enough fruit. We went in the other direction and planted one each of 24 different varieties, so we enjoy regular apple tastings and usually have enough fruit on hand for fresh eating, applesauce, or apple pie.

Rootstocks for an Apple Hedge

An apple espalier should have full-dwarf rootstocks or super-dwarf rootstocks. Below are a few that work well for apple hedges. For suppliers, see "Apple Sources," page 110.

EMLA 26—Most of our trees grow on EMLA 26 rootstock, which some pomologists would regard as too vigorous for an espalier because it makes 12- to 15-foot trees. But our goal is to produce both fresh fruit for the table and grafting scions for our nursery business, so the vigorous growth of EMLA 26 is not a problem. Think twice about using this stock unless you are willing to do considerable pruning.

M-9/EMLA 111—An interstem (double) graft that produces a tree similar in size to EMLA 26. Here a cutting from the unrooted stem of an M-9 rootstock is grafted onto an EMLA 111 root. Then a cutting from a desirable variety is grafted onto the M-9 interstem. This arrangement dwarfs the tree because the interstem restricts the sap flow from the vigorous EMLA 111 root, which normally produces a 20- to 25-foot tree. M-9/EMLA 111 combination stocks are often more expensive than other types, but they are well anchored and vigorous.

BUD 9—A Russian rootstock that grows to about 10 feet. We have several trees on BUD 9, and they seem to be exceptionally hardy. Their moderate growth makes for a well-proportioned look and easy pruning.

M-9—Probably the most widely planted full-dwarf rootstock; it produces a tree that grows to 10 feet, but it is susceptible to fire blight.

CG-16—A new release from Cornell, similar in size to M-9 but showing superior fire blight resistance.

P-22—This super-dwarf rootstock, developed in Poland, produces trees that are smaller than those on M-9, topping out at about 6 feet. P-22 roots are exceptionally winter hardy.

M-27—A 1929 cross of Malling 13 and EMLA 9, this super-dwarf rootstock is great for home gardeners who need compact trees for small spaces. Varieties on M-27 are appreciably more dwarfed than those on M-9. Trees yield heavy crops the second year after planting.

Apple Sources

FINDING ORCHARDS IN YOUR AREA
Apple Journal
www.applejournal.com/trail.htm

Pick Your Own
www.pickyourown.org/statelist.htm

TIPS FOR HOME ORCHARDISTS
North American Fruit Explorers
www.nafex.org

Home Orchard Society
www.homeorchardsociety.org

APPLE TREES FOR HOME ORCHARDS
Adams County Nursery, Inc.
26 Nursery Road
P.O. Box 108
Aspers, PA 17304
717-677-8105
www.acnursery.com
About 70 varieties of antique and modern apples; range of rootstocks

Big Horse Creek Farm
P.O. Box 70
Lansing, NC 28643
www.bighorsecreekfarm.com
More than 300 varieties of apples, including custom-grafted antique and heirloom trees

Calhoun's Nursery
295 Blacktwig Road
Pittsboro, NC 27312
919-542-4480
Specializing in antique southern varieties

Century Farm Orchard & Nursery
1614 Rice Road
Reidsville, NC 27320
336-349-5709
More than 450 varieties, particularly old southern apples

Cummins Nursery
4233 Glass Factory Bay
Geneva, NY 14456
315-789-7083
www.cumminsnursery.com
Heirloom and disease-resistant apples; cider varieties; custom-grafted trees

Fedco Co-op Garden Supplies
P.O. Box 520
Waterville, ME 04903
207-873-7333
www.fedcoseeds.com/trees.htm
About 30 varieties that originated in Maine, almost all on standard (nondwarfing) rootstocks

Greenmantle Nursery
3010 Ettersburg Road
Garberville, CA 95542
707-986-7504
Antique apples, pears, peaches, and plums

Henry Field's Seed and Nursery
P.O. Box 397
Aurora, IN 47001-0397
513-354-1494
www.henryfields.com

Raintree Nursery
391 Butts Road
Morton, WA 98356
360-496-6400
www.raintreenursery.com

Stark Bro's Nurseries
P.O. Box 10
Louisiana, MO 63353
800-478-2759
www.starkbros.com
*Limited selection of varieties on dwarf and
semidwarf rootstocks*

St. Lawrence Nurseries
325 State Highway 345
Potsdam, NY 13676
315-265-6739
www.sln.potsdam.ny.us
*150 apple varieties for Zones 3 to 4, including
many antiques, all on extremely hardy, vigorous,
standard-size Antonovka rootstocks*

Trees of Antiquity
(formerly Sonoma Antique Apple Nursery)
4395 Westside Road
Healdsburg, CA 95448
805-467-2509
*About 140 varieties of organically grown
antique apples and other fruits*

Urban Homestead
818 Cumberland Street
Bristol, VA 24202
276-466-2931
Antique and modern apple trees

Vintage Virginia Apples
P.O. Box 210
North Garden, VA 22959
434-297-2326
www.vintagevirginiaapples.com

SOURCES OF HEIRLOOM FRUITS
Applesource
1716 Apples Road
Chapin, IL 62628
800-588-3854
www.applesource.com

Kilcherman's Christmas Cove Farm
11573 N. Kilcherman Road
Northport, MI 49670-9722
231-386-5637
www.applejournal.com/christmascove/index.html

Lakeside Orchards
318 Readfield Road
Manchester, Maine 04351
207-622-2479
877-453-7656
www.maine.com/apples/Welcome.html

Tree-Mendus Fruit Farm
9351 E Eureka Rd
Eau Claire, MI 49111
269-782-7101
www.treemendus-fruit.com

For More Information

GROWING APPLES

The Apple Grower: A Guide for the Organic Orchardist, by Michael Phillips
Lots of good growing and marketing information for home orchardists.
Chelsea Green, 1998

The Backyard Orchardist, by Stella Otto
A thorough guide to starting and maintaining a small orchard.
OttoGraphics, 1995

Temperate-Zone Pomology,
by M.N. Westwood
The most comprehensive resource for home gardeners with some science background; out of print but widely available used.
Timber Press, third edition, 1993

IDENTIFYING APPLES

Apples, by Roger Yepsen
More than 200 varieties depicted in watercolors, along with descriptions of their taste and uses.
W.W. Norton, 1994

Apples: A Catalog of International Varieties, by Tom Burford
A handy guide describing more than 300 varieties.
Available from the author (P.O. Box 367, Monroe, VA 24574), 1991, revised 1998

Apples for the 21st Century,
by Warren Manhart
The eating and storage qualities, genetic history, cultivation, and disease resistance of 50 cultivars.
North American Tree Company, 1995

The Book of Apples, by Joan Morgan and Alison Richards
A wide-ranging history of apples briefly profiling more than 2,000 varieties.
Ebury Press, 1993

The Fruits and Fruit Trees of America,
by Andrew Jackson Downing
See page 13.
John Wiley, 1850; available used in reprints

Fruit, Berry and Nut Inventory, by Kent Whealy and Joanne Thuente
See pages 19–20.
Seed Savers Exchange, third edition, 2001

Old Southern Apples, by Creighton Lee Calhoun Jr.
The southern fruit sleuth's bible, describing over 1,600 varieties of apples.
McDonald & Woodward, 1995

CIDER

Cider: Making, Using, and Enjoying Sweet and Hard Cider, by Annie Proulx and Lew Nichols
Instructions for everything from planning an orchard to building and using a cider press.
Storey Publishing, 2003

Contributors

Tom Burford is an orchard and nursery consultant specializing in restoration, re-creation, and design at historic sites and private estates. He is the author of *Apples: A Catalog of International Varieties* (1991, 1998), a reference work on hundreds of apples, and has written manuals on grafting, orchard design, and fruit-tree culture. Burford, a Virginia native, presents workshops and seminars nationally and continues to explore for "lost" fruit varieties worldwide.

Ed Fackler founded Rocky Meadow Orchard & Nursery in New Salisbury, Indiana, in 1975 and operated it until 2000, when it was acquired by Gardens Alive. He is currently the director of horticulture research for Gardens Alive. Fackler cowrote *Fruit Grafters Handbook* (2001) with Tom Burford and contributed to the Brooklyn Botanic Garden handbook *Growing Fruits: Nature's Desserts* (1996). He has also written articles for *Fine Gardening* and other magazines. He is a past president of North American Fruit Explorers and the Indiana Horticulture Society.

Beth Hanson is former managing editor of Brooklyn Botanic Garden's handbooks and editor of eight BBG handbooks, including *Designing an Herb Garden* (2004), *Natural Disease Control* (2000), *Chile Peppers* (1999), and *Easy Compost* (1997). She also contributed to *The Brooklyn Botanic Garden's Gardener's Desk Reference* (1998). She lives outside New York City and writes about gardening, health, and the environment for various publications.

Tim Hensley runs Urban Homestead in Bristol, Virginia, a mail-order nursery specializing in antique apples. The father of eight children, he has written for a variety of publications including *Mother Earth News, Grit, Highlights for Children, Fine Gardening, Homelife, Old-House Journal,* and *Smithsonian*.

Ian A. Merwin is a pomologist at Cornell University, where his current research projects include screening apple rootstocks for resistance to soil-borne diseases; integrated pest management systems for orchard weeds; collecting germplasm of European bittersweet cider apples; and molecular fingerprinting techniques to study soil microbial populations in the apple tree root zone. He and his wife grow new and antique apple varieties on their farm for their local farmers' market and for making fermented ciders.

Curt Rom grew up in northwest Arkansas, the son of a pick-your-own orchardist and research pomologist. He is an associate professor of horticulture and fruit crops at the University of Arkansas, in Fayetteville, where he concentrates on fruit crop management and physiology, tree fruit cultivar testing, and the university's fruit-breeding program. His current research efforts are directed at small-scale, multiple fruit crop farming systems and the development of organic horticulture technology. He is past president of the American Pomological Society and is an avid gardener.

Ted Swensen is a retired professor from Portland Community College, in Portland, Oregon, where he taught general biology, botany, and organic gardening. He now runs Prima Consulting, a small business for organic growers and home gardeners. He is past president of the Home Orchard Society and editor of the quarterly publication *Pome News*. His home sits on a 65- by 75-foot city lot, where he raises 65 apple trees, 5 cherry trees, and 3 fig trees, as well as grapes, blueberries, and currants.

Illustrations

Roger Yepsen pages 34, 40, 44, 45, 52, 58, 61, 67, 71

Steve Buchanan pages 93, 97, 98, 99, 101

Tim Hensley Collection pages 11, 18, 21, 22 both, 65, 86

Emma Skurnick page 98 (pruning tools)

Photos

David Cavagnaro cover, pages 25, 55, 63, 91, 94, 103 bottom

Derek Fell pages 2, 70, 103 top

Irene Jeruss pages 4, 15, 19, 26, 47, 53, 64, 68

Thomas Jefferson Foundation/ Leonard Phillips page 9

Walter Chandoha pages 16, 20, 80, 88, 102

Jerry Pavia pages 30, 108

David Karp pages 31, 32, 33, 35, 36, 38, 39, 41, 43, 46, 48, 49, 51, 54, 57, 62, 66, 69, 83, 85

Matthew Wyne pages 35, 79

Jules Janick pages 42, 72, 84

Alan & Linda Detrick pages 56, 74, 75, 96

Ian A. Merwin pages 59, 60, 76, 77

Philip L. Forsline/USDA, ARS, Plant Genetic Resources Unit page 78

Ted Swensen page 105 both

Tim Hensley page 107

USDA Hardiness Zone Map

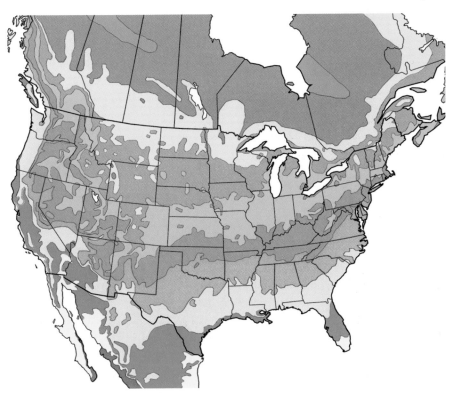

Zones and Minimum Winter Temperatures (°F)

Zone 1 below −50°

Zone 2 −50° to −40°

Zone 3 −40° to −30°

Zone 4 −30° to −20°

Zone 5 −20° to 10°

Zone 6 −10° to 0°

Zone 7 0° to 10°

Zone 8 10° to 20°

Zone 9 20° to 30°

Zone 10 30° to 40°

Zone 11 above 40°

Index

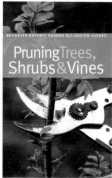

More Information on Growing Fruits

Growing Fruits: Nature's Desserts contains everything you need to start your own backyard orchard, with tips on how to site, plant, and prune apples, pears, peaches, raspberries, and grapes, as well as rare and ornamental fruits.

Pruning Trees, Shrubs, & Vines takes the guesswork out of snipping, sawing, and slicing as it introduces you to the fundamentals of plant growth and explains the essential techniques for all major pruning tasks.

Ordering Books From Brooklyn Botanic Garden

World renowned for pioneering gardening information, Brooklyn Botanic Garden's award-winning guides provide practical advice for gardeners in every region of North America.

Join Brooklyn Botanic Garden as an annual Subscriber Member and receive three gardening handbooks, delivered directly to you, each year. Other benefits include free admission to many public gardens across the country, plus three issues of *Plants & Gardens News, Members News,* and our guide to courses and public programs.

For additional information on Brooklyn Botanic Garden, including other membership packages, call 718-623-7210 or visit our website at www.bbg.org. To order other fine titles published by BBG, call 718-623-7286 or shop in our online store at www.bbg.org/gardengiftshop.